❊

Seeing with the Eyes of Love

❊

Seeing with the Eyes of Love

REFLECTIONS
ON A CLASSIC
OF CHRISTIAN
MYSTICISM

*by Eknath Easwaran
with an Afterword
by Carol Flinders*

NILGIRI PRESS

©1991 by The Blue Mountain Center
of Meditation. All rights reserved
Printed in the United States of America
Text designed, printed, and bound by Nilgiri Press
ISBN : cloth, 0–915132–65–6; paper, 0–915132–64–8

First printing July 1991

The Blue Mountain Center of Meditation,
founded in Berkeley, California in 1961 by Eknath
Easwaran, publishes books on how to lead the spiritual
life in the home and the community.

For information please write to
Nilgiri Press, Box 256,
Tomales, California 94971

Printed on recycled, permanent paper

♾ The paper used in this publication meets the
minimum requirements of American National Standard
for Information Services – Permanence of Paper for
Printed Library Materials, ANSI Z39.48–1984

Library of Congress Cataloging-in-Publication Data
will be found on the last page of this book.

Table of Contents

Introduction

In my state of Kerala there is a Christian tradition going back nearly two thousand years. The Apostle Thomas, one of Jesus' direct disciples, is believed to have come to the coast of Kerala and founded a Christian community there, which would mean that Christianity came to Kerala well before it came to most of Europe. In my college classes there were students from these ancient Christian families, looking golden-brown and dark-eyed like the rest of us and carrying the same surnames, but with first names like David, Joseph, and Peter.

However, these Christian communities are concentrated in the coastal part of Kerala, around Cochin and Travancore. My village was inland, so I don't think I had any exposure at all to the message of Christ until a Christian teacher joined the faculty of my high school. My Uncle Appa, our schoolmaster, invited him regularly to our ancestral home, and I imagine my interest in the teachings of Christ was probably first kindled by meeting this man. Not long afterwards, I left home for college – a Catholic college located some fifty miles from my village – and there I met an individual who to my mind lived out those teachings perfectly.

The headmaster of my college was Father John Palakaran, a Catholic priest from a distinguished Kerala Christian family who had taken his degrees at Edinburgh University. English, French, Latin, Greek,

Sanskrit, Malayalam – in all of these he was fluent. He was a brilliant scholar, though he carried it so lightly it wasn't until years later that I realized the extent of his erudition. Father John always wore his black academic robes in the classroom. He had a deep, resonant voice, and he smoked the kind of large cigars that would become the trademark of the film star Edward G. Robinson.

The overall impression was intimidating, and as a sixteen-year-old Hindu boy fresh from the village, I was intimidated rather easily. From the very beginning, though, I sensed that this man lived for his students, and in return I gave him my utmost respect. I had a class with him just one hour a week during that first year, and I used to sit in the front row lost in admiration. I had never heard English spoken so sonorously, with such wonderful broad *a*'s. I wanted to sound just like that!

Father John was able to see that I was having a hard time when it came to speaking English. I could read it well, and write it too, but I had never spoken English before. When the instructors asked a question, I had to frame my answer in Malayalam first and then translate it into English. By the time my answer was ready, the discussion had moved on. This was thoroughly upsetting to me, because in high school I had been an excellent student.

That first year was difficult for me in another way too: I had never been away from home before. The college officials must have realized that would be the case for most of their first-year students, because they did not bring us into dormitories yet. Instead we were lodged with local families, where we could eat our meals and be treated almost as if we were at home. It was a good way to ease the transition into college life, but nonetheless I was homesick quite a lot of the time.

Father John began to understand my difficulties. His way of helping me learn to speak English was to encourage me to enter the college debate program. I wanted to do everything I could to please him, and that gave me the motivation to work extremely hard. He wasn't in the habit of paying compliments, and that didn't trouble me since my grandmother wasn't either. Instead, he supported me in quiet ways. Every now and then, for example, guessing what it would mean to me, he used to call me into his private study to talk – not in his office but in his own rooms, which were part of what we called "The Bishop's Palace." He had a handsome study in the Victorian mode, and because I held him in such esteem I would look all around to see what kind of pictures were on the wall, what books he kept on the shelf – everything. His academic robes would be hanging in the corner during these visits; he would be wearing his simple white cassock.

I remember him calling me there one afternoon after he had heard me speak in class. We chatted a while and then he asked casually, "Did you have breakfast?"

"Yes, Father," I said, rather bewildered by the question. "I had a good breakfast."

"Well, then, *if* you had a good breakfast," he said, leaning forward full of intensity, "why did you swallow the last words of every sentence?"

It was not a question he would have to ask me twice!

It was about a year later when one of his assistants came to me in class and said, "Father John wants you."

I hurried to his rooms and found him reclining in an armchair with his feet up, puffing an after-lunch cigar.

"You have probably heard there is an intercollegiate debate coming up." I had. I knew it covered the whole region and that it was the most prestigious debate we could compete in – and that it was for Catholic colleges only. Since I wasn't Catholic, I hadn't even thought about participating.

"I want you to represent this college."

I was overwhelmed – I literally couldn't believe it. And what if I let him down? I must have muttered something to that effect because he cut me off with a gesture. "I'll be the judge of whether you are equal to it," he said. "I'm not consulting you."

My eyes filled with tears. When I could finally speak I started to ask, "If I fare badly . . ."

He cut me short with a cheerful shrug. "Just don't come back!"

To my great relief I found that none of the students appeared to resent Father John's decision to send a Hindu boy to represent a Catholic college – in fact, when my debate partner and I left for the event, a crowd of our schoolmates came to the train station to see us off. Still, I felt quite out of place and alone. The debate was held in a big, crowded auditorium, and besides probably all being Catholic, all the other contestants seemed to be wearing European suits.

At the end of the day, to my surprise, the panel of judges not only gave me and my partner the intercollegiate trophy; they gave me first place for individual elocution. By the time we reached our campus that night the news had preceded us, and hundreds of students met our train and followed as we carried the trophy to the Bishop's Palace.

Father John opened the door and looked at me. "So you've come back," he said.

During the four years I spent at college, without calling attention to what he was doing, Father John managed to work a great transformation in me. He helped me find confidence, but detachment as well. I was so grateful that I kept a picture of him in my room. And, inevitably, rumors got back to my village: I was said to be on the verge of becoming a Catholic. My granny only smiled. She knew that it wasn't a creed or religion I was drawn to, but the sheer nobility of the man himself.

I never considered converting, and nothing in my relationship to Father John ever made me think he expected me to. I'm sure he gave me books, for I must have been as curious about his religious background as I was about every detail of his life. He may even have given me *The Imitation of Christ*. But I was young, and my interests – encouraged by him – were wide. I had not yet reached the point where religious literature had any personal meaning for me.

In fact, it wasn't through books at all, but through the lives of individuals like Father John that the message of Christ first reached me. I have had the good fortune to know quite a number of Christian men and women like him, both Protestants and Catholics, who lived truly selfless lives. Such individuals are indeed the lamp "set high for all men to see" of which Christ spoke. Long before I took to the spiritual life myself, they helped me understand that the selfless life of which all the world's scriptures speak is also a life of beauty.

The actual writings of the world's great spiritual teachers – from the Hindu, Christian, Buddhist, Sufi, and other traditions – did not draw me until I began to practice meditation. I was a college professor by then, so when the ground began to shift beneath my feet – when all the things I had valued and worked for were no longer enough to satisfy my deepest longings – it was natural to turn to books in search of an explanation. I looked through all the texts on psychology that I could lay hands on, but none of them shed light on what was happening to me. Only when I began to read the works of the great mystics did the ground begin to feel more solid beneath my feet.

Initially, of course, I was most at home with the mystics of Hinduism and Buddhism. But gradually I became conversant with those of the Christian tradition as well. The inspired poetry of John of the Cross enthralled me, and I found Teresa of Avila's writings on meditation vivid and practical. Reading Meister Eckhart and Jacob Boehme, I found myself wondering whether they might not somehow have dipped into the Upanishads. During this period, one figure began to intrigue me more and more – not because I knew anything about his life, but because the work he had produced – *The Imitation of Christ* – seemed to me to hold a unique place in Christian mystical literature.

It's difficult to say when I first came across the *Imitation*, but I remember the thrill of certitude that its composer was a man of deep spiritual awareness. I found it to be a practical guide to developing spiritual awareness. I could see right away why Swami Vivekananda, a direct disciple of Sri Ramakrishna and founder of the Vedanta Society, had traveled to the West with the Bhagavad Gita in one pocket and *The Imitation of Christ* in the other. It is the special strength of a few books, and this is one of them, that down through the ages they have helped bridge the gap between cloister and household. Though the *Imitation* was composed in a monastic setting, its teachings are universally applicable, and they have been treasured by Protestants as well as Catholics, laypersons as well as monastics.

To explain its appeal is not simple. The autobiographical elements that make Augustine or Teresa of Avila so accessible are absent. Though the language is very apt and dignified, there are no poetic or visionary flights like those we find in John of the Cross or William Blake. For theological brilliance you would have to look elsewhere. Much of *The Imitation of Christ* is no more dazzling than a manual for woodworkers. But then, if you really want to know about carpentry, you don't *want* a manual that will dazzle; you want one that will tell you how to make a miter joint, how to use a skill saw, and what the best finish is for a tabletop. *The Imitation of Christ* is just that kind of book – an entirely practical manual for sincere spiritual aspirants.

The great mystics of all religions agree that in the very depths of the unconscious, in every one of us, there is a living presence that is not touched by time, place, or circumstance. Life has only one purpose, they add, and that is to discover this presence. The men and women who have done this – Francis of Assisi, for example, Mahatma Gandhi, Teresa of Avila, the Compassionate Buddha – are living proof of the words of Jesus Christ, "The kingdom of heaven is within." But they are quick to tell us – every one of them – that no one can enter that kingdom, and discover the Ruler who lives there, who has not brought the movements of the mind under control. And they do not pretend that our own efforts to tame the mind will suffice in themselves. Grace, they remind us, is all-important. "Increase in me thy grace," Thomas prays, "that I may be able to fulfil thy words, and to work out mine own salvation."

The hallmark of the man or woman of God is gratitude – endless, passionate gratitude for the precious gift of spiritual awareness. Universally, from whatever tradition they come and no matter how long and hard they struggled, they agree that without divine grace no one can achieve what they have achieved. At the same time, they tell us divine grace is not something that descends at particular times and places, like lightning. Rather, it surrounds us always. Like a wind that is always blowing, said Francis de Sales; like fire, said Catherine of Genoa, that never stops burning: "In this world the rays of God's love, unbeknownst to man, encircle him all about, hungrily seeking to penetrate him."

It can be baffling, this mysterious interplay of divine grace and individual effort. The truth is, both are absolutely necessary. "Knock," Jesus assured us, "and it shall be opened unto you," and he keeps his promise. But we have to knock hard. We have to sound as if we mean business. And before we can do that, all our desires must be unified. This comes in stages, in cycles repeated over and over – the painful effort, then the breakthrough to a new level of awareness; again the effort, again the breakthrough. Sometimes it can feel like we're doing it all ourselves, but in the final stages all doubts fall away, and we realize we were in His hands from the very start. The moment we feel even the slightest attraction to the spiritual life – the moment when we first take a book on meditation off the bookstore shelf – divine grace has called, and we have answered.

In the West, the practice of meditation has been associated so persistently with the cloister that ordinary men and women haven't readily taken it up. "We don't have time," they say. Sometimes they add, "Besides, isn't meditation just an attempt to run away from life's challenges?"

When we look at the lives of the great mystics, however, we find ready proof that turning inward does not mean turning away from life. For the man or woman "in the world but not of it," just as well as for monks or nuns, action and prayer are the two halves of the spiritual life, as complementary as breathing in and breathing out. In prayer and meditation, we breathe in deep; in the outward action of selfless service we breathe out again, blessing the lives of those around us in meeting life's challenges head-on. This does not require a special gift. Just as each of us has been born with the capacity to breathe, we have all come into life with the capacity to draw upon the deep spiritual resources released through meditation and make a great contribution to life.

In reading *The Imitation of Christ* and commenting on it to men and women of today, I have had to come to terms with certain elements that strike the modern mind as negative. These are not unique to medieval Christianity: you can find them in other religions too.

To take one example, I have never responded favorably to descriptions of hell. To my mind, an angry mind or an envious heart is its own hell. Where traditional language might speak of sins and punishment, I speak instead, less dramatically, of mistakes and consequences.

Again, medieval writers in particular – and ascetics of all religions in general – like to use the arresting language of condemnation and subjugation. They speak, for example, of "this *vile* body of ours," and tell us we "must *mortify* the flesh." To me the body is not vile, but a useful and long-suffering friend. Here Saint Francis himself comes to my rescue when he addresses the body as "Brother Donkey." He says, in effect, "I feed him and take care of him, but I ride on him; I don't let him ride on me!" Today, instead of talking about "mortifying" the body and senses to bring them under control, I always speak of training them – bringing body and senses to their optimum condition, like an athlete in training.

The heart of *The Imitation of Christ,* and certainly the part that is best known, is the fifth chapter of Book III, called traditionally "The Wonderful Effects of Divine Love." It seems to me to distill the essential teachings not just of Thomas a Kempis, but of Christianity itself.

Readers who love the thirteenth chapter of First Corinthians – "Though I speak with the tongues of men and of angels" – will hear echoes of it throughout this chapter. Readers familiar with the writings of Saint Bernard and Saint Augustine will identify still other echoes and reworkings of loved passages. Was Thomas a Kempis cribbing? No, but he would be the first to tell us that the *Imitation* is not the product of anyone's imagination or poetic inspiration. He signed the book only at the very end, as a copyist would have. It was habitual among the Brothers of the Common Life, Thomas's spiritual family, to keep notebooks where the monks would jot down particularly inspiring passages from Scripture or the church fathers, or even sayings and homilies received from one another. One or more of these compilations was undoubtedly the basis for the *Imitation*. Since Thomas himself made no strong authorial claim, there is no need for us to quibble over which parts of the text are "really" his. In fact, Thomas summed up the question himself, neatly, early in the *Imitation* where he wrote, "Let not the authority of the writer offend thee, whether he be of great or small learning; but let the love of pure truth draw thee to read. Search not who spoke this or that, but mark what is spoken."

"The Wonderful Effects" is a soaring hymn of love that stands perfectly well on its own. But when its position in *The Imitation of Christ* is understood, it becomes doubly interesting because it marks a sharp turning point in the text. Books I and II have been quite sober in tone – searching, serious, and very down to earth. Up to this moment only one voice has been heard, that of the seasoned spiritual teacher addressing an audience of newly dedicated aspirants – novitiates, perhaps. He has laid out for them the basic terms of the spiritual life: what will be expected of them and what the disciplines are that they are undertaking.

Book III opens in a different vein altogether. Gone is the counselor and guide of Books I and II. We hear a voice now that is altogether new: the clear, ringing voice of someone who has absorbed well the lessons of the preceding books, and now seeks nothing in life but to become united with the Lord. Each of us, clearly, is meant to identify ourselves with this aspirant. His first words echo the Psalmist: "I will hearken what the Lord God will speak in me." Ardently, again and again, he calls out, "Speak, O Lord, for thy servant heareth. . . . Incline my heart to the words of thy mouth: let thy speech distill as the dew." Over and over he declares his readiness to be taught – no longer by scripture, but from within. And at last, a voice replies: "My son, hear my words, words of greatest sweetness. . . . My words are spirit and life." From this moment on, *The Imitation of Christ* is a dialogue, and an indisputably mystical treatise.

Tools for Transformation

Since I will be referring to meditation throughout this book, I need to say a few words about just what I mean by the term.

When I talk about meditation I am referring to a specific interior discipline which is found in every major religion, though called by different names. (Catholic writers, for example, speak of "contemplation" or "interior prayer.") This interior discipline is not a relaxation technique. It requires strenuous effort. It does dissolve tension, but in general, especially at the beginning, meditation is *work*, and if you expect to find it easy going, you'll be disappointed.

Second, meditation in this sense is not a disciplined reflection on a spiritual theme. Focused reflection can yield valuable insights; but for the vast majority of us, reflection is an activity on the surface level of the mind. To transform personality we need to go much, much deeper. We need a way to get eventually into the unconscious itself, where our deepest desires arise, and make changes *there*.

So what *is* meditation? It is the regular, systematic training of attention to turn inward and dwell continuously on a single focus within consciousness, until, after many years of daily practice, we become so absorbed in the object of our contemplation that while we are meditating, we forget ourselves completely. In that moment, when we are empty of ourselves, we are utterly full of what we are dwelling on. This is the central principle of meditation: we become what we meditate on. "Write thou my words in thy heart," says the Lord in Chapter 3 of Book III, "and meditate diligently on them."

Here is a brief summary of the form of meditation I follow, and a still briefer summary of seven other practices which support and strengthen your meditation during the day. (There is a much fuller presentation in my book *Meditation*.) Together these comprise a complete eight-point program for spiritual living, which I have followed myself for almost forty years. I warmly invite you to join me while you are reading this book!

1. Meditation

* Choose a time for meditation when you can sit for half an hour in uninterrupted quiet. Early morning is best, before the activities of the day begin. If you wish to meditate more, add half an hour in the evening, but please do not meditate for longer periods without personal guidance from an experienced teacher.

* Select a place that is cool, clean, and quiet. Sit with your back and head erect, on the floor or on a straight-backed chair.

* Close your eyes and begin to go *slowly*, in your mind, through the words of a simple, positive, inspirational passage from one of the world's great spiritual traditions. (Remember, you become what you meditate on.) I recommend beginning with the Prayer of Saint Francis of Assisi:

Lord, make me an instrument of thy peace.
Where there is hatred, let me sow love;
Where there is injury, pardon;
Where there is doubt, faith;
Where there is despair, hope;
Where there is darkness, light;
Where there is sadness, joy.

O divine Master, grant that I may not so much seek
To be consoled as to console,
To be understood as to understand,
To be loved as to love;
For it is in giving that we receive;
It is in pardoning that we are pardoned;
It is in dying to self that we are born to eternal life.

You will find it helpful to keep adding to your repertoire so that the passages you meditate on do not grow stale. "The Wonderful Effects of Divine Love" is an excellent choice. My book *God Makes the Rivers to Flow* contains many other passages that I recommend, drawn from many traditions.

* While you are meditating, do not follow any association of ideas or allow your mind to reflect on the meaning of the words. If you are giving your full attention to each word, the meaning cannot help sinking in.

* When distractions come, do not resist them, but give more attention to the words of the passage. If your mind strays from the passage entirely, bring it back gently to the beginning and start again.

* Resolve to have your meditation every day – however

full your schedule, whatever interruptions threaten, whether you are sick or well.

Meditation is never practiced in a vacuum. Certain other disciplines always accompany and support it, varying somewhat according to the needs of a particular culture or audience. Here are the remaining seven disciplines I have found to be enormously helpful in supporting the practice of meditation.

2. Repetition of the Holy Name

Meditation involves use of a memorized passage, and it requires that one sit quietly. The Holy Name, on the other hand, can be repeated under almost any circumstances, and it is so brief – a spiritual formula, really – that it will come to your mind under even the most agitating circumstances. (In fact, that is often just when you will want it!)

Repetition of the Holy Name is a practice found in every major religious tradition. Many Christians simply repeat *Jesus, Jesus, Jesus.* The desert fathers repeated the Prayer of Jesus, which in the Orthodox tradition is used even today: *Lord Jesus Christ, have mercy on me.* Catholics repeat *Hail Mary* or *Ave Maria*, and one Catholic monastic friend has written to inform me that she uses an ancient Aramaic formula: *Maranatha*, "Come, Lord Jesus." Choose whichever version of the

Holy Name appeals to you; then, once you have chosen, stick to that and do not change. Otherwise you will be like a person digging little holes in many places; you will never go deep enough to find water.

Repeat the Holy Name whenever you get the chance: while walking, while waiting, while doing mechanical chores like washing dishes, and especially when you are falling asleep. Whenever you are angry or afraid, nervous or hurried or resentful, repeat the Holy Name until the agitation in your mind subsides.

Do not make up your own version of the Holy Name, but use a formula that has been sanctioned by centuries of devout tradition. If you repeat it sincerely and systematically, it will go deeper with every repetition. It can be with you even in the uttermost depths of your consciousness, as you will discover for yourself when you find it reverberating in a dream – or, deeper still, during dreamless sleep.

3. Slowing Down

Hurry makes for tension, insecurity, inefficiency, and superficial living. To guard against hurrying, start the day early and simplify your life so you do not try to fill your time with more than you can do. When you find yourself beginning to speed up, repeat the Holy Name to help you slow down.

It is important here not to confuse slowness with

sloth. In slowing down we attend meticulously to details, giving our best even to the smallest undertaking.

4. One-pointedness

Doing more than one thing at a time divides attention and fragments consciousness. When you read and eat at the same time, for example, part of your mind is on what you are reading and part on what you are eating; you are not getting the most from either activity. Similarly, when talking with someone, give that person your full attention. These are not little things – taken together they help to unify consciousness and deepen concentration. One-pointed attention is a powerful aid to meditation.

Everything you do should be worthy of your full attention. When the mind is one-pointed it will be secure, free from tension, and capable of the concentration that is the mark of genius in any field.

5. Training the Senses

In the food we eat, the books and magazines we read, the movies we see, all of us are subject to the dictatorship of rigid likes and dislikes. To free ourselves from this conditioning, we need to learn to change our likes and dislikes freely when it is in the best interests of those around us or ourselves. We can begin by saying no when our senses are urging us to indulge in something that is not good for our body or mind. The senses are the secretaries of the mind; to get the mind to listen to us, we need to bring them over to our side.

6. *Putting Others First*

Dwelling on ourselves builds a wall between ourselves and others. Those who keep thinking about *their* needs, *their* wants, *their* plans, *their* ideas, cannot help becoming lonely and insecure. When we learn to put other people first, beginning within the circle of our family and friends and co-workers, we deepen our own security and dramatically enrich our relationships.

It is important to remember here that putting others first does not mean making yourself a doormat, or saying yes to whatever others want. It means putting the other person's *welfare* before your own personal desires. That is what love is: the other person's welfare means more to you than your own. And love often requires you to say no.

7. *Spiritual Reading*

Our culture is so immersed in what the mass media offer that we need to balance our outlook by giving half an hour or so each day to spiritual reading: something positive, practical, and inspiring, which reminds us that the spark of divinity is in all of us and can be released in our own lives by meditation, prayer, and daily practice. Just before bedtime is a good time for this kind of reading, because the thoughts we fall asleep in will be with us throughout the night.

8. Spiritual Association

When you are trying to change your life, you need the support of others with the same goal. If you have friends who are meditating along the lines suggested here, you can get together regularly to share a meal, meditate, and perhaps read and discuss your spiritual reading. Share your times of entertainment too; relaxation is an important part of spiritual living!

Chapter One

Ah, Lord God, thou holy lover of my soul,
when thou comest into my heart, all that is
within me shall rejoice. Thou art my glory
and the exultation of my heart: thou art
my hope and refuge in the day of my
trouble.

Thomas a Kempis does not say "O thou Tripartite
Unity" or "Ah, Supreme Godhead and Ultimate
Being," but "thou holy lover of my soul." His Lord is
his intimate companion, his beloved sweetheart, who
can be seen, heard, touched, even tasted, in the aspirant's
heart of hearts. Thomas's writings, like the entire medieval period, are permeated with the beautiful understanding that the Lord of Love is not an abstraction at all
– that, in the words of Julian of Norwich, "He is our
clothing, for he is that love which wraps and enfolds us."

None of the great mystics of the period – or of any
other time – will claim that this perfect intimacy can be
attained swiftly or easily, any more than in an ordinary
romance. Before we can become one with the Beloved
there are mountains in consciousness to be climbed,
fierce rivers to be forded, epic inner battles that must be
fought and won. Yet, just as great worldly romances
often begin with a single, telling glance, so, very often,
does this one. Suddenly, for no rhyme or reason, deep
within you something stirs. "When thou comest into

my heart," says Thomas, "all that is within me shall rejoice." For a split second, it seems, you catch a glimpse of Someone. It may take no longer, in the words of one mystic, than an "Ave Maria." But in that brief, glowing instant, the doubts and uncertainties of a lifetime can vanish. And suddenly the direction of your life changes.

When this experience came to the scholarly Saint Augustine, he sighed in profound relief, "No further would I read, nor needed I." And down the ages, every scholar turned aspirant has sighed with him – including Thomas a Kempis, who writes in the opening chapters of the *Imitation:* "What have we to do with genus and species, the dry notions of logicians? He to whom the Eternal Word speaketh is delivered from a world of unnecessary conceptions."

This experience is the same whether it comes to Saint Augustine in the last days of the Roman Empire, to Thomas a Kempis in medieval Europe, or to Mahatma Gandhi in British India. The truths of the spiritual life hold true for all times. Yet each period in history, each culture, imparts its own cast to the discovery of God. In our times – more than ever in history, I believe – the emphasis of civilization is on the external world. It is as if we were content to spend all our time decorating the outside of a house – the lawn, the shrubs, the trellis and the porch swing – without ever going inside, without even looking for the One who is waiting there. We never so much as knock on the door. Teresa of Avila put it very well: "It is no small pity and should cause us no little shame that through our own fault we do not understand ourselves or know who we are . . . we only know we are living in these bodies and have a vague idea . . . that we possess souls. All our interest is centered on the rough setting of the diamond, the outer wall of the castle – that is to say, on these bodies of ours."

If there is a God, we reason, he is surely outside, as is everything else that catches our attention. Vaguely, fondly even, we imagine as we go about our business that Someone is probably keeping an eye on us – like Agatha Christie's Inspector Poirot, seated bundled up in a trench coat on the Orient Express, peering out obliquely from behind the Paris edition of the *Herald Tribune*. To the murmurings from within, meanwhile – the faint stir and rustle of a presence deep inside of us, and a voice hauntingly beautiful – we turn a deaf ear. "We stuff our ears and say we cannot hear you," complained the medieval German mystic Hans Denk. "We close our eyes and say we cannot see you."

The external world, so fascinating, so glamorous, has us firmly in hand and thoroughly mesmerized. Lasting happiness is almost ours, it promises – over there, just ahead of us, right around the next corner. When we round that corner and find that happiness has eluded us, something in us says, "It's just around the *next* corner." Our life becomes a continual pilgrimage around corners. Yet such is human credulity that even after rounding a thousand corners, we still say, "The thousand and first, *that* is the one!"

As long as we believe that we are happy only when some external condition is fulfilled, so long – even when that condition *is* fulfilled – will there be the proviso "Now let *another* condition be fulfilled." It is this habit, this almost mechanical fixation of the mind, that keeps us forever chasing down blind alleyways.

But what if you get tired of looking outside? What if you decide to look within? Back you go to that house for a closer look! Now you're not so interested in the flowers in the garden or the Victorian porch swing. You are looking for a door, and you find it. And from behind it, if you press your ear against the panels, you can hear a voice, faint but vibrant: "The kingdom of heaven is within." And so is the King; so is the Queen.

Once you have made the decision to turn inward, you begin to look differently at life. Your mounting need is like a powerful searchlight, intently focused. Up to now you have trained its bright light onto material satisfactions, and finally pierced right through them. You have trained it on prestige and power with the same result. Finally, thoroughly dissatisfied, in a magnificent sweep of spiritual intuition you turn the searchlight within. And this is when it takes place: that split second of astonished certainty when you *know* that the Lord lives within you.

Afterwards you want nothing more in the world than to repeat the experience. You want with all your heart to gaze again into those compassionate eyes and remain longer in that healing presence. So you do just what any ordinary lover would do: you try to go back to the place where you saw your beloved last. Not a café or a library or a tennis court now, but deep within your own consciousness. It is not easy to find your way back, and nearly impossible to remain there for long at a time. But every human being has the capacity to do this; every one of us can discover the Christ within and be united with him forever. The door to deeper consciousness might seem to be locked except to saints, but we do have a key, every ordinary one of us: the practice of what Catholic mystics call interior prayer, which I call meditation.

To enter deeper levels of consciousness through meditation, we need to train our very capacity to attend. All our mind, all our desires, all our will, must be fused. In the end, this is the purpose of all the legitimate spiritual practices that have come down to us in the great religions of the world; but the most effective way I know of is to meditate sincerely and systematically on a memorized spiritual passage. If you can sit in silence, eyes closed, going through the words of the Lord's Prayer with such complete concentration that you don't even hear the lawn mower next door, your journey inward is well underway.

But of course it isn't enough to be underway; you have to know where you're going. You need a map, and this is the second reason to meditate on a deeply spiritual passage. The Lord's Prayer, the Beatitudes, the Prayer of Saint Francis, Saint Teresa's "Let nothing disturb thee" – all these are passages deeply imbued with Christ-consciousness. They are soaked with his love and dyed deep in his wisdom, and as you let each word sink into your heart in meditation, you cannot help but draw closer to the source, the Christ within. You can almost hear his voice: "Over here! You're getting warmer!"

Nothing but your own growing dissatisfaction –

your sharpening hunger for meaning and permanence and abiding truth – can so challenge the hold of the world that you turn inward like this and hear for yourself the very personal invitation of Jesus Christ: "Knock, and it shall be opened; seek, and you shall find; ask, and it shall be added unto you." When Thomas a Kempis declares, "Thou art my glory, and the exultation of my heart: thou art my hope and refuge in the day of my trouble," he is celebrating precisely this discovery: that real glory and exultation, true hope and refuge, can be found nowhere but in union with the Lord, who is within.

In every time and every place where people have thought deep and hard about life, they have left some record of the feelings I've been describing, usually in symbol and myth. They describe a haunting sense of being in exile, of being a wanderer far from home. Chronic homesickness would seem to be as categorically human as the opposable thumb.

According to the Judeo-Christian tradition, it is Eden we long for – a garden home where our every need was met and we were complete. Somehow, for reasons we can't remember, we were turned out. The memory haunts us, undercutting every ordinary satisfaction, and we wander through life growing more and more hungry, feeling alienated in the world, always on the lookout.

To carry the metaphor a little further, we are all tourists in this world – looking about ourselves, trying to figure out what we ought to be feeling when we stand before this statue or that palace, and wishing at every turn that we were "back home." Just eavesdrop sometime on a Grayline bus tour. I remember in India you could hear them murmur to each other, "Well, it's certainly not like this back home," or "George, don't you wish we could be having dinner *back home* tonight?" The nostalgia of world travelers is ironic, because it is usually a feeling very like nostalgia that has launched them in the first place: something about the brochures at the travel agent's, the pictures of swaying coconut palms that beckon so seductively, that makes us want to say, "There, that's where I'll find my paradise. That's what I've always yearned for." We each have our own versions. To some it's the arched ways of Oxford University, to others the gleaming white islands of the Aegean. "There – *there* I could be happy."

Emigrants all, we know very well that we are meant to live in permanent joy and ever-increasing love, and nothing short of this will satisfy us. In the words of Mechthild of Magdeburg, "The soul is made of love, and must ever strive to return to love." There is an inward tug in everybody, a persistent voice that calls, "Come back to the source." When Thomas calls the Lord "my hope and refuge in the time of my trouble," he reminds us that we are all refugees, far, far away from our homeland.

Thou art my hope and refuge in the day of my trouble.

Even in the most intimate relationships, it is seldom that one person can remain steadfast when the other is irritated or in a depression. It takes boundless love on the part of the Lord to say, "When everything is going well with you, I understand that you might well forget me. But when things are wrong with you, when the clouds are gathering and looking dark on the horizon, why don't you come to me *then*?"

Who but the great lover would say this? No human being with any self-respect would allow himself to be a last resort, but Jesus is always willing. He says, "When everything has failed – when your bank has gone bankrupt and your bar has gone bar-rupt, when all friends have forsaken you and even your dog won't wag his tail for you – come to me then. I will never turn you away."

That is how dear we are to him. When we are tardy, when we delay our return to him by being selfish and self-willed, it is he who grieves. "Look at my kids! They're still stumbling down blind alleys in a far country." In a magnificent Bengali proverb, it is said that the Lord is always waiting for us with his arms open wide; and for every step we take towards him, he takes seven towards us.

Whether we like it or not, one day we are going to leave our blind alleys and begin to search for him. Nobody is ever lost; nobody ever ceases to be a child of God. When people come to cry on my shoulder because life is not making them happy, I say, "Don't get my jacket wet. That's not going to help you. Why not let me show you how to leave this country altogether? You're ready to emigrate!" You may have traveled far and wide – to China, Tibet, Uzbekistan – but that is all horizontal travel, just moving about from one point on the physical plane to another. When the urge to turn inward becomes importunate, you are ready for *vertical* travel – ready to go deep within yourself in search of the divine.

Getting ready for this inward journey is a lot like preparing for a trip to India or Japan. You may start by reading about it. World travelers, you know, drop in at the travel agency and pick out a number of pamphlets from that attractive rack on the wall; then, if they get interested, they get books from the library and start reading about local customs. Here, too, you get enthralled reading the itineraries of the great travelers in the lands of the spirit: Augustine, Teresa, the Compassionate Buddha, all of whom say in much the same language, "The land of joy and love is within." And they don't talk about the places they've been the way horizontal travelers like John Gunther or Paul Theroux do. Horizontal travelers enjoy *differences:* different food, different customs, different ways of dress. But vertical travelers rejoice in unity. External differences are interesting for a while, but the human being's deepest need is for discovering what unites us all.

So you read, and you plan; and then slowly you begin to get serious about making the journey. You try to balance your budget by curtailing certain expenses here and economizing there. By staying home from movies you don't need to see and keeping away from the sales, you will be able to pay your travel expenses. And just as if you were going to a third world country where health conditions are not the best, you've got to get certain shots. They are not very pleasant. But you are so eager to visit the country, you have read so much about it, that you say, "Let's go and get it over with." You even manage a wry grin.

Now you have your medical certificate, and you're ready for your passport. But here, in this very important matter of identification, there is a big difference between traveling outside and traveling inside. With horizontal travel, of course, you have to get your passport at the outset. With vertical travel, you get it at the very end of the journey. The purpose of a physical passport is to establish your identity in the limited, physical sense: Who were your parents? Where were you born? Do you have any moles? But in the deeper sense, establishing your real identity is the whole object of traveling inward.

And let's not forget the important question of luggage. You won't be allowed to take all you want – just forty pounds, no more. So you select only what is essential. You find a lot of things you can do without. Ultimately you know you may have to carry your own bags, so you try to keep them light and portable.

This is the story of getting started in the long inward journey of meditation. Every traveler who has seen the heaven within, who has become a resident in what Augustine calls the City of God, will describe to you how difficult the journey is, how terribly challenging the conditions. But at the same time, all these voyagers will tell you how determined they were. There was nothing else in life they wanted.

The mystics don't deny the existence of the external world; it is we who deny the *internal* world, which they are telling us is every bit as real. There are mountains in the world within, they tell us, higher than the Himalayas. You remember that the great English climber George Leigh Mallory, when journalists asked why he wanted to climb Mount Everest, gave a very British reply: "Because it is there." Similarly, if you ask the mystics why they want to travel inwards, they will tell you, "Because God is there."

Many of you, I imagine, have ancestors who braved danger and hardship to make their home in a new land. If you could ask them what it was like, say, a hundred and fifty years ago to travel from the East coast to the West, they would tell you stories that would give you nightmares. Yet they didn't go back to Poughkeepsie or Pittsburgh; they just kept on. It is the same in meditation. "This act of will [*determinación*] is what he wants of us," says Saint Teresa in her autobiography. Nothing less will get us where we need to go.

Chapter Two

But because I am as yet weak in love,
and imperfect in virtue, I have need to
be strengthened and comforted by thee;
visit me therefore often, and instruct me
with all holy discipline.

To travel deep into consciousness through the practice of meditation you must have a huge desire, so huge it swallows up all your other desires. The onset of that desire is a sure mark of divine grace. Often it begins as a nagging, driving restlessness. To be content no longer with picking up what is floating on the surface of life, but to want only the pearls on the bottom of the sea: that is the touch of grace.

With this desire, however, comes a terrible responsibility. You know now that you must begin the long, arduous task of training the mind and senses through spiritual disciplines. Nobody has to tell you this, for the awareness wells up from deep inside. A great saint from the Russian Orthodox tradition, Theophan the Recluse, stated it unequivocally: "The principal condition for success in prayer is the purification of the heart from passion, and from every attachment to things sensual."

I had always understood there to be a connection between spiritual awareness and certain disciplines that train the mind and senses, and for that very reason I had wanted nothing to do with the spiritual life. I imagined my body being bent with prayer and fasting, my intellect clouded with speculation, and my life deprived of health, happiness, color, and friendship.

In a sense my fears were justified, for the path to spiritual awareness is as steep and fearsome as any the human being has ever attempted. But what I could not have foreseen was how joyfully I would set out upon that path when the moment to do so actually came. That is because the desire to gain mastery over one's mind and senses does not come from some distant deity or even from a monastic rule. It comes from deep within yourself – from the Lord of Love within. Catherine of Genoa describes this experience beautifully:

> When God sees the soul pure as it was in its origins, he tugs at it with a glance, draws it and binds it to himself with a fiery love that by itself could annihilate the immortal soul. In so acting, God so transforms the soul in him that it knows nothing other than God; and he continues to draw it up into his fiery love until he restores it to that pure state from which it first issued.
> . . . That is why the soul seeks to cast off any and all impediments, so that it can be lifted up to God.

The thrust toward God-consciousness starts as a vague stirring – just a *tug*, as Catherine says – and grows little by little until in the final stages it is a relentless pull like the outgoing tide. That it makes itself known at all is an expression of grace, sheer grace; but how rapidly it grows depends entirely on how you and I respond. And our response, the great mystics of all traditions point out, is almost always a matter of overcoming our own self-will. This is the heart of the spiritual life for a long, long time. *Naughting* is the medieval Christian's term for what is really the aim of all spiritual disciplines: the reduction to absolute zero of everything in us that is selfish and separate.

In that sense, it's nothing extraordinary that Thomas a Kempis is asking from us here. We all have the desire for this journey; all he asks is that we feed that desire. Whenever you have a lesser desire, the practice of meditation will enable you to siphon the energy away from that desire and channel it into this tremendous wanderlust. The City of God is within. You can reach it here and now, in this very life, through the practice of meditation.

It is a demanding adventure, a difficult undertaking, but we have come into this life for nothing else. In the inspiring words of Meister Eckhart, "Man shall become a seeker of God in all things, and a finder of God at all times and everywhere, and among all people, and in every way."

Thomas has addressed the Lord in beautifully intimate words. Now he explains why he must ask his help:

> *But because I am as yet weak in love, and imperfect in virtue, I have need to be strengthened and comforted by thee . . .*

So many people have come to me during the last thirty years and confessed tragically, "I don't think I have the capacity to love. I'm not strong enough to form a lasting, loving relationship. I don't think I'm a bad person; I just don't know how to love."

I ask them, "Have you always known how to write?" They say no.

"Have you always known how to read?" They say no.

"But now you are able to do both. How did you manage that?"

"Well, I studied. I practiced a lot."

We have only to look at little children learning to write. Just to write *cat,* their whole face participates in the effort – brows knitted together, lips twisted, tongue sticking out. Look in again twelve years later and there they'll be on the university campus, where a learned professor is indulging in words of thundering sound, with lightning playing about his head. There will be that same child, scribbling furiously and not missing a syllable. This is what practice does, and it is the same with love. It requires unremitting practice. There is nothing wicked in not being able to love. You just haven't learned to read the book of love or write in it. You haven't mastered the skill.

So when Thomas a Kempis confides to the Lord, "I am weak in love, and imperfect in virtue," he is saying, "Come teach me. Come help me. I need this skill desperately; for I can see that my own capacity to love is but a drop compared with the ocean of love I have glimpsed in you." And this is just what the Lord has been waiting to hear. "God is bound to act," says Meister Eckhart, "to pour himself into thee as soon as he shall find thee ready." No one expects to learn tennis just by thinking about it, or calculus, or windsurfing. If you're serious, you'll put aside time for practice. It is the same with learning to love. It takes time.

To give yourself that time, there is one simple step that anyone can take – simple, but enormously effective. Just get up an hour earlier in the morning. Throughout the day, you will feel the difference. You have ten minutes more now to spend over breakfast with your family, ten minutes longer to get to your workplace without cursing stoplights along the way, and five minutes' leeway to chat with your co-workers when you get there.

Five minutes here, ten there, can add up to a significant change. You don't find yourself sneaking desperate looks at your watch now, and you're no longer jerked about from place to place, always just in time or a few minutes late. It's in those fresh new intervals, at the breakfast table, in the office, that you find countless little opportunities to give your attention and affection to those around you – not in one dramatic episode, but in small encounters throughout the day.

To get up earlier, you will probably want to go to bed a little earlier too. That won't come easily. For me, it meant making an honest reassessment of how I was spending my time. I sat down and wrote a list of all my obligations – my committee memberships, the concerts I liked to attend, the learned societies I had joined. Then I just started drawing lines through the ones that could be deemed inessential. I braced myself for my colleagues' reaction: "E.E.'s withdrawing! He's not pulling his weight!" But to my amazement, my presence was not missed as keenly as I'd expected. This was briefly disappointing, but soon the payoff came. Here was an hour, there was half an hour. I had more time now to really look at my students, my family, my fellow faculty members – time to really listen to them.

Of course, slowing down the day is only the first step. The hurried pace that keeps us "weak in love" originates in the mind. You might stop at someone's desk to be sociable, but that doesn't mean your *thoughts* have stopped. They are immaterial, after all! Most people are perceptive enough to know when this is taking place. If you're pretending to chat with them while your mind has sprinted ahead toward the conference room, you might as well take the rest of you there too.

No one can love with a mind that is going fast – or one that is divided. No one can love with a mind that is apt to swerve wildly, whether to avoid the small exigencies of daily life or to pursue something bright across the room that attracts you.

Let me suggest a small experiment. For a day or so, think of yourself as James Joyce, or any other writer who specializes in stream of consciousness writing. With the uncritical eye of the motion picture camera, observe your thought processes when you are in different states of mind. When you are feeling irritable, take a peek. If you have occasion to be afraid or anxious, check again. If a strong desire overtakes you and you can manage to see what's going on in the mind, take note. Check your vital signs at the same time: see how rapid your pulse is, and whether your breathing is shallow and quick, or deep and slow.

If you can do this accurately – which is harder than it

sounds – you will make a very interesting discovery. Fear, anger, selfish desire, envy: all these are associated with a speeded-up mind, and when the mind speeds up, it takes basic physiological processes with it. The thinking process hurtles along, thoughts stumble over one another in an incoherent rush – and, on cue, the heart begins to race and breathing becomes quicker, shallow, and ragged.

Interestingly enough, the reverse is also true. Once the mind gets conditioned to speed, not only do speeding thoughts make the body go faster, speeded-up behavior can induce negative emotions as well. Suppose you've slept through the alarm and are in a rush to get off to work. You rip through the kitchen like a whirlwind, grabbing whatever you need as you go, trying to button your shirt while you eat your toast on your way out the door.

The next time you catch yourself like this, watch and see how prone your mind is to negative responses. Everything seems an obstruction or a threat. Your children look hostile – if you see them at all – and even the dog seems out to ruin your day, draping herself right across the threshold in the hope of tripping you up. "Watch out!" the kids say once you're gone. "It's going to be another of those mean-mood days."

In a way, getting through the day is much like driving a car. When you're driving over sixty-five miles per hour, you need a lot of space just to turn or stop. At high speeds you can't see the scenery along the way; if you try, you may get yourself killed. You might even miss the road signs, and if a possum or squirrel is trying to cross the road, you have no choice but to run it down. In the same way, those who have been conditioned to race and hurry through life often don't see people, just blurs. When they hurt others, they are often not even aware of it. They can injure relationships without even knowing that damage has been done.

A speeding mind is a dangerous thing. When thoughts are going terribly fast, they are out of control, and there is no space between them. To press the analogy further, it's like those dangerous moments on the freeway when cars are not only speeding but following bumper to bumper. Everyone is in danger.

A thrilling realization comes when you begin to understand this two-way relationship between speeded-up thinking and negative emotions. If you are chronically angry, fearful, or greedy, you know well how much damage these tendencies have done to your relationships, making you "weak in love and imperfect in virtue." And you know, too, how dauntingly hard they are to change when you approach them head-on. Their roots go deep in your past conditioning. You can talk them out, analyze them in your dreams, reason with yourself, go to anger workshops and fear seminars – still they wreak havoc, out of control.

But suppose that instead of going after chronic anger or fear directly you were to tackle the thought process itself – the mind in its Indianapolis speedway mode. When a car is going a hundred miles per hour, you can't safely slam on the brakes. But you *can* lift your foot off the accelerator. From one hundred miles per hour the speed drops to ninety-eight, then to ninety-five, then ninety, until finally you're cruising along at a safe and sane fifty-five. You've decelerated gradually and safely.

This is exactly what happens to the mind in meditation. You put your car into the slow lane – the inspirational passage – and you stay there, going through the words of the passage as slowly as you can. Distractions will try to crowd in, and you may need to pick up the tempo just a bit. You don't want to leave big gaps for them to rush into. For the most part, though, you just increase your concentration. In this way, little by little, you can gain complete mastery over the thinking process.

Saint Francis de Sales describes the process in more traditional language:

> If the heart wanders or is distracted, bring it back to the point quite gently and replace it tenderly in its Master's presence. And even if you did nothing during the whole of your hour but bring your heart back and place it again in Our Lord's presence, though it went away every time you brought it back, your hour would be very well employed.

As you do this, your health cannot help improving, because the poor, innocent body is typically the victim of ungoverned mental activity. When I see somebody in a burst of fury, to my eyes it almost looks like a thousandth of a heart attack. When it's repeated over and over, when you get angry more and more easily, the time may come when the heart will say, "I can't take it any longer!" Of course, it might not be the heart; it might be the lungs or the digestive organs or some other physiological system or process. Whatever the result, I believe the same contributing cause is often involved: a chronically agitated mind weakening the health of the body.

People who don't easily get provoked, on the other hand, have what one researcher, Suzanne Kubasa, calls a "hardy personality." It is difficult to upset them, difficult to make their mind race out of control. As the mind slows down, I would say, you get more hardy – more patient, more secure, more healthy, more resilient under stress. Meditation is the key to achieving this end.

Visit me therefore often . . .

In the Gospel According to Matthew, Jesus gives his disciples instructions in how to pray. Not in public, for everyone to see,

> But thou, when thou prayest, enter into thy closet, and when thou hast shut thy door, pray to thy Father which is in secret, and thy Father who seeth in secret shall reward thee openly.

I have always suspected that Jesus had a still deeper meaning in these lines, and I was pleased to find on reading some of the Russian mystics that they felt the same way. By "in thy closet," I think Jesus was trying to suggest that real prayer takes place in the heart, and that is exactly what the great teacher Theophan the Recluse believed. "Outward prayer alone is not enough," he insists. "God pays attention to the mind, and they are no true monks who fail to unite exterior prayer with inner prayer." To sequester oneself is only the first step – for real prayer to take place, we must shut out every external distraction and travel deep inward.

Mystics down the ages have issued a consoling assurance: when you turn to God, they say, God is turning to you. Eckhart says, in words stamped with the authority of his experience:

> You need not seek him here or there; he is no further off than the door of your heart. There he stands lingering, awaiting whoever is ready to open and let him in. You need not call to him afar; he waits much more impatiently than you for you to open to him. He longs for you a thousandfold more urgently than you for him – one point, the opening and the entering.

The Lord is always at home deep inside each one of us, and he is always ready to greet us there. If time stretches long between visits, it's no fault of his. We are the ones who are delaying by postponing the practice of the spiritual life. "God is near us, but we are far from him," says Meister Eckhart. "God is within; we are without. God is at home; we are in the far country."

To visit the Lord, or let him visit us, we must enter the depths of consciousness through meditation. To receive the benefits of his loving instruction, we don't have to make a shopping list, keep it in our meditation room, and say, "Lord, I lack *(a)* patience, *(b)* endurance, and *(c)* forgiveness. So please give me *(a)* patience, *(b)* endurance, and *(c)* forgiveness." You don't have to ask for these virtues because in the practice of meditation, you become what you meditate on. When your attention is completely focused on the words of the passage, the words slowly begin to write themselves on your consciousness. They are no longer being heard by the ears, or read by the eyes, or even being understood by the intellect, they are starting to be etched on your heart.

At the very instant you are praying with Saint Francis, "Lord, make me an instrument of thy peace," the Lord is doing just that – by teaching you to conduct yourself in your daily life with love and respect to everyone, whatever they say to you or do to you. You are transforming your consciousness and conduct in the image of Saint Francis.

People say to me, "Oh, but surely this is only possible for great saints!" Much the same thing must have been said to William Law, the great Anglican devotional writer who was a contemporary of Pope and Swift, because he takes it up with deft eighteenth century irony: "It will perhaps be thought by some people that these hours of prayer . . . ought not to be pressed upon the generality of men who have the cares of families, trades, and employments; and that they are fitting only for monasteries and nunneries."

The argument is familiar, and we've all heard it: "Meditation is a good idea for people who have time – that is, for those who have nothing better to do."

But Law counters it. Prayer is not placed before us as a duty, he says, but "recommended to all people as the best, the happiest, and the most perfect way of life. For people, therefore, of figure, or business, or dignity in the world to leave great piety and eminent devotion to any particular orders of men, or such as they think have little else to do in the world, is to leave the kingdom of God to them."

The effects of deepening meditation can be seen all through the day. Your concentration improves and your vision becomes twenty-twenty. Where you could see only blurs before, now you see forms and faces. You can read the delicately phrased messages that are written in the eyes of others. "My daughter looks worried about something – I'd better help her talk about it." Or even, "The dog! He's reminding me I didn't play with him last night . . . " You don't hurt people now, and even if they hurt you, you are less likely to retaliate in anger – because you can see the whole picture. You see all the factors in the lives of those around you that are influencing their behavior.

As the rush of thinking slows down, there comes a little space between two thoughts. If someone does something to provoke you, it's not that you don't feel angry, or are not aware of what the other person is doing, but now you can slowly open out an interval between two angry thoughts – half a car-length, then two, then three. Traffic thins out, so the danger of collision is lessened. You have moved out of the fast lane, where anger hurtles along, and you have dropped into the slow lane – the one where positive emotions like patience, kindness, and goodwill travel. The physiological benefits are many, and immediate. When your thoughts slow down, your lungs breathe more deeply and your heart beats more slowly.

. . . *and instruct me with all holy discipline.*

But meditation alone is not enough. You can make great progress during a morning's meditation only to see it all undone at the breakfast table, when someone admits to having dented a fender slightly or overdrawn the checking account. To hold on to the precious advances you make in meditation, and to extend the effects of meditation into the rest of the day, you need to practice certain supporting disciplines as well. In one form or another, though the emphasis will vary with time and circumstance, these disciplines are universal. They are undertaken wherever men and women are striving to still the mind and transcend narrow, individual consciousness.

The first of these is the use of the Holy Name, called the *mantram* in the Hindu tradition. Meditation is going inside to pay a formal visit to the Lord who lives in the depths of consciousness: you sit down and politely give him your undivided attention. Repeating the mantram, by contrast, is quite informal, though never casual. There are times throughout the day and night when you need to draw on the Lord for love or wisdom or strength, and you need to do it *right now*, regardless of where you are or what you are doing. Through the repetition of a simple spiritual formula like *Ave Maria*, the Prayer of Jesus, or just the name of Jesus alone, you can do just that. You're not paying a visit in person; you can't even afford the price of a phone call. Instead, you're calling the Lord collect. A wave of fear or anger is about to overtake you, or a great wave of selfish desire, and you just go out for a brisk walk repeating *Jesus, Jesus, Jesus* in your mind. The rhythm of your breathing will blend with the rhythm of your footsteps. Soon you will find that the rhythm of your mind has slowed down too, and its turbulence has subsided.

The power of this simple discipline has been laid out eloquently by the anonymous author of the *Cloud of Unknowing:*

> . . . a naked intent directed unto God, without any other cause than himself, sufficeth wholly. And if thou desirest to have this intent lapped and folden in one word, so that thou mayest have better hold thereupon, take thee but a little word of one syllable, for so it is better than two; for the shorter the word, the better it accordeth with the work of the spirit. Such a word is this word G O D or this word L O V E. . . . And fasten this word to thy heart that so it may never go thence for anything that befalleth. This word shall be thy shield and thy spear, whether thou ridest on peace or on war. With this word thou shalt beat on this cloud and this darkness above thee. With this word thou shalt smite down all manner of thought under the cloud of forgetting; insomuch that if any thought press upon thee to ask what thou wouldst have, answer with no more than this one word. . . .

When people say or do harmful things to you, you can almost see the cloud of darkness forming across your mind. It is this cloud that covers over your need to give and forgive, and it can seem as thick as a great thunderhead. But with the mantram you can just beat on that cloud until you disperse it and drive it away, and there behind it, shining like the sun, is the capacity to forgive others and draw them closer to you. It isn't always that you forget the wrongs that have been done or said, but there is no longer any emotional charge.

The use of the Holy Name is a powerful tool for deepening spiritual awareness. It is not to be confused with the practice of meditation, but when we recite the Holy Name to ourselves during the day, it allows us to draw upon the resoluteness and calm of our morning's meditation.

It is time now to turn to a discussion of the aspects of the spiritual life that are more difficult to fit gracefully into our lives. We've discussed the value of meditation and the mantram in some detail. And the place and value of the disciplines of slowing down and one-pointed attention are apparent enough – learning to do just one thing at a time makes obvious sense in the context of meditation, and so does slowing down. Reading the great mystics and keeping spiritual companionship need little explanation: after all, if you're trying to become a great bowler, you seek out the company of bowlers and read books by master bowlers on how to bowl; that is all very reasonable and straightforward. But the remaining two disciplines in this eight-point program require real artistry to fit into our lives. They are skills that we learn only with trial and error after faithful effort. But to make our lives a work of art, we eventually have to master these difficult disciplines: training the senses and putting others first.

Invariably at my weekend retreats someone asks why I put so much emphasis on training the senses. It is almost always a very fresh-faced young someone, who is still enjoying the wide margins that nature gives to youth – the iron digestion, the resilience to bounce right back after an all-night party or cram session, the ears that can tolerate one-hundred-twenty-decibel rock bands without flinching. Older people are a little more reticent – rather as if life itself had suggested that some degree of mastery over the senses can be helpful. I address the question in two ways.

First, I point out that training the senses is not an end in itself. Indeed, the senses have no life of their own. They are just the mind's connection with the outside world, the channels through which impressions of the world pour into the mind, keeping it endlessly busy and active. Medieval writers spoke of the senses as our "wits," for they are our means of *knowing*. The more varied and exciting the impressions are, the higher is the level of activity. Day and night, awake and dreaming, the mind is like the engine of a car that has been left running, consuming fuel and running down the battery.

"The eye hath not its fill of seeing, nor the ear of hearing," said the prophet of Ecclesiastes. This is where the trouble starts, for the senses are wonderful servants but poor masters. And as long as the mind is searching outward for satisfaction, the senses are likely to be in control, and the mind will follow their lead. The palate will say, "Let's eat a third piece of pie," and the mind will mutter, "Yeah, okay, sure, go ahead." You can see who's running the show. Before the mind can turn inward, to receive what is there and ready to be given, it has to become still; but the senses have to be won over first.

The mind itself is more than a match for us. But where the senses are concerned, we have a fighting chance, and in coming to grips with them, we sharpen the skills, the wit, and cunning it will take to go after the mind itself – in due time.

To put it more affectionately, I like to think of the mind as the Big Boss and the senses as his five secretaries. In any bureaucracy it's difficult to go directly to the boss. If he's a busy man – and the mind is nothing if not busy! – with lots of appointments and high-level negotiations on his hands, you are wise to start by trying to win the good will of the secretaries. At first they are chilly and inhospitable, and for a long time the situation resembles those Hollywood movies of the 1930s where Spencer Tracy or Clark Gable breezes into an office, flings himself onto the corner of the receptionist's desk, and inquires, ignoring her icy looks, "Hey, honey, how's the boss man today?" But gradually, just as in those highly predictable screenplays, the ice melts and the secretary becomes a staunch ally. She'll warn you, "He's there and I'll send you in, but watch your step; he's eaten three salesmen for breakfast!"

Winning over the senses, however, requires more than Hollywood charm. In collusion with the mind, they've been having the run of our life for a long time now, and they're not about to give it up.

Which brings us to the second part of my reply. Training the senses, I always emphasize, does not mean mortifying them. The senses are naturally *servants* of consciousness, not enemies. They are meant to serve us well; it is just that they've been badly raised. They are unschooled. "Why do you behave so terribly?" we ask in exasperation. And all they can say in response is "I can't help it!"

The senses are being stimulated all the time. Every billboard screams that satisfaction lies outside. No one can help getting caught in that belief, and a lot of vital energy is trapped in living it out. I was no exception. But today, after many years of exacting discipline, I can count on my senses never letting me down. They might drop delicate hints about that chocolate mousse on the pastry cart, but a firm "Careful!" brings them right back to the fresh strawberries. I have their complete, joyful cooperation now – but the victory hasn't come easily.

The palate, indeed, is the ideal starting point for getting some mastery over your senses. You have five, six, a *dozen* opportunities every day: breakfast, lunch, dinner, and any number of between-meal snacks! No need to talk of fasting or strange diets. Just resolve to move away from foods that don't benefit your health and begin choosing foods that do. With this simple resolution, you'll strengthen your will and deepen your meditation – and please your physician, too.

I first became interested in changing my diet for the better under the influence of Mahatma Gandhi, when he was writing weekly articles for his paper *Young India.* One week he would write about the struggle for Indian independence from British rule, the next week about village uplift, and the third week about the value of goat's milk. Diet was an important topic for him, and he experimented all his life to discover the very best. Indians can be quite traditional about food; they always want the dishes that "mother used to make." But Gandhi put tradition aside in favor of health, and his example appealed to me deeply.

I too, of course, had been brought up on Indian cuisine – first Kerala style, later Central Indian. And I had enjoyed it all thoroughly. It never occurred to me to ask what the purpose of food is. Gandhi's example prompted me to ask; and I concluded, to my great surprise, that food is meant to strengthen the body. So I started changing. I began to eat fruits and vegetables that wouldn't have appealed to me in earlier days at all. As I began to focus more on health, I found that I enjoyed salads, and that highly spiced curries no longer seemed palatable. I was prepared now to agree with Gandhi's dictum that taste lies in the mind.

On the other hand, far-reaching though these changes were, I don't think I really understood what Gandhi was getting at until much later, when I began to meditate. It was then that I made what was for me a remarkable discovery. When I needed a lot of drive to go deeper in meditation – for example, if I had a problem to solve that required more energy and creativity than usual – I found that I had only to pick a strong sensory urge and defy it. When you suddenly need cash, don't you go and shake the piggy bank? It was a little like that. I would look around intently to see what kind of cravings I had, and then I would walk up to a really big one and say, "Come on – because I am really broke." The desire would come on strong, and I would push it back and come out with both my pockets loaded.

My whole outlook on desire changed. Formerly, when a strong urge would come, I used to do what everybody does: yield to it, and not reluctantly either. Now I began to rub my hands with joy at the prospect of doing just the opposite. "Here's another desire! It's strong, so I'll gain even more by defying it." I began to understand that any strong desire, when it is defied, generates a lot of power. It's like watching the needle on your gas gauge go up! But I must confess to you that this insight did not come to me because of my own ingenuity. It came because of my teacher's blessing. I could almost feel her looking on and smiling as I recklessly flung aside one after another of these fetters and plunged ahead.

Not every desire, I should say, is to be rejected out of hand. I distinguish very carefully between harmless desires and desires that are harmful to the body or mind – or, of course, to those around you. If the desire is for food that is wholesome, you may well be able to yield with full appreciation. But if it is a desire for something sweet that you don't need, you will find you can get equal satisfaction out of refusing it. It's a deceptively simple change in perspective. Your attitude toward the body becomes very different: you see it no longer as an instrument of pleasure, but as an instrument of loving service.

From the very start, you will be able to see some benefits in training the senses. But the full reward comes only after long years of meditation in conjunction with the allied disciplines. For when the senses and the mind become still, we realize our true nature in the supreme climax of meditation. Saint Teresa of Avila describes this supreme state with an inspired simile:

As soon as you apply yourself to prayer, you will feel your senses gather themselves together. They seem like bees which return to the hive and there shut themselves up to work at the making of honey. And this will take place without effort or care on your part. God thus rewards the violence which your soul has been doing to itself, and gives to it such a domination over the senses that when it desires to recollect itself, a sign is enough for them to obey and so gather themselves together. At the first call of the will, they come back more and more quickly. At last, after countless exercises of this kind, God disposes them to a state of utter rest and of perfect contemplation.

Our senses are groping into the external world just like bees hovering over a fragrant garden. What restaurant can I go to? What show can I see? What store is having bargain sales? At least the bees' busy search will be rewarded, but for us, as we grow more sensitive, there is only bitter disappointment; for there is no nectar in the outside world. No honey is being manufactured there; all the honey is being made inside.

Thomas a Kempis has confessed to being "weak in love and imperfect in virtue." Now he opens his heart more deeply still. In the next verse he admits to being under the sway of "evil passions" and "inordinate affections."

Chapter Three

*Set me free from evil passions, and heal
my heart of all inordinate affections; that
being inwardly cured and thoroughly
cleansed, I may be made fit to love,
courageous to suffer, steady to persevere.*

Most of us, I think, will hesitate here and say, "'Evil
passions' might be putting it just a little too strongly.
Emotional difficulties? Yes, we do have a few. A problem with anger? Yes, we can confess to that. Towering
rage has gripped us on occasion. Nameless fears do torment us more often than we'd like, and jealousy is not
unknown to us, we admit. But still, isn't that word *evil* a
little extreme? A little . . . *medieval?*"

When Thomas a Kempis says "evil," however, he is
not asking us to wallow in guilt. Rather he is saying,
"Hey, you'd better take these characters seriously.
They mean business! They're out to get you!" The most
ruthless hijackers can't hold us hostage more effectively
than our own passions when they take over our lives. At
international airports today every effort is made to be
sure we don't have dangerous traveling companions,
and you and I have to make the same careful inquiries
where our thoughts are concerned. The fellow behind
dark glasses, with the folded newspaper under his arm –
look out! Interpol has a fat file on him. Don't take him

with you! And that nice-looking elderly lady? That's no bag of knitting she's got draped over her arm!

Tempestuous passions like fear, anger, and greed aren't born six feet tall and armed to the teeth. They usually start as little, little fellows. You begin to dwell on an angry thought, something provoking, a genuine injustice done to you. At first it's just a little mouse gnawing at your consciousness with very small teeth. You keep on dwelling on it, though, feeding it every day by giving it more and more attention, until finally it becomes the mouse that roared. In Thomas a Kempis's own description: "For first there cometh to the mind a bare thought of evil, then a strong imagination thereof, afterwards delight, and an evil motion, and then consent. And so by little and little our wicked enemy getteth complete entrance, whilst he is not resisted in the beginning."

When we're trying to grasp a phenomenon as elusive as the mind, metaphors are exceedingly helpful. So we can think of thoughts as traveling companions – or, if we return for a moment to the language of the automobile, we can think of Thomas a Kempis's "evil passions" as cars hurtling along the freeway at top speed, too close to one another for safety. In fact it is the same thought, repeating itself over and over and over again: *Ihatehim-IhatehimIhatehimIhate. . . .* If we could look more closely, we would see a break between each repetition; but as long as the mind is going so fast, we don't see the break, so we identify ourselves with the compulsive thought. Since there is no opening in traffic for another kind of thought – like compassion, or courage – to come in, we are at the mercy of the one recurring motif.

Meditation is the key to setting all this right. By gradually slowing down our process of thinking, we can come to see the intervals, tiny as they are, between one angry thought and the next. Little by little, as we bring our mind back again and again to the words of the passage, we extend those intervals – and new possibilities arise. During the rest of the day, by repeating the Holy Name whenever a wave of fear or anger arises, we strengthen this process of disidentification.

In other words, through the practice of meditation, you can gradually learn to disidentify yourself from the powerful emotions that can turn on you and wreck your life. That powerful emotion of *I hate him, I hate him* is not *you;* it's a dangerous terrorist who has hitched a ride on your plane. Once you can pull back even a hair's breadth from a big wave of anger or greed and say, "That's not really me," you've as good as snatched the hijacker's weapon right out of his hands.

. . . and heal my heart of all inordinate affections . . .

Again, "inordinate affections" has a quaint sound to it, like something out of an Aristotelian treatise on poetics. For a contemporary translation, you might substitute "addictions" or "compulsive attachments." Thomas's language may be quaint, but his message is very up-to-date. He is implying that desire, which is our capacity for love, is spilling out all the time. Belgian chocolate ice cream bars or "recreational drugs," fine wines or hand-crafted jewelry – every one of these represents a little hole in consciousness where love is ebbing out. Unchecked, this constant leakage will finally drain the reservoir, leaving you with an empty tank and miles from home. To find your real Self, you need every drop of the fuel that is desire. That is why it is so important to plug all those little holes one by one.

A compulsive desire is like any other thought over which you have no control. It flows continuously: *I want that, I want that, I want that,* with no space between the demands. But when you begin to deepen your meditation, two things happen. First, of course, the thought process itself slows down. Second, you develop a new kind of attitude toward desires. You get a taste of the powerful satisfaction that comes when you go against long-standing compulsions. You realize that you don't have to identify with those strong urges. Hesitantly, you begin to oppose some of them.

After a while, when a very strong, powerfully compulsive desire overtakes you and your mind just keeps chanting *I want that,* you catch sight of a tiny opening between the demands. It's only a split second in duration at first, but in time it grows long enough for another thought, another *kind* of thought, to make itself known. "Hmmm . . . maybe part of me *does* want that. Maybe part of my mind. But do *I*? Is it really in my long-term best interest to gratify this desire? Or my family's?"

When this happens, you are on the way to developing a supremely precious skill: when a desire comes of which you do not approve, you can draw your mind back. It is almost like reaching out, taking hold of its collar, and pulling it back gently. The desire will quietly vanish, but it will leave you heir to all the energy that fueled it. I began by saying, remember, that training the senses is not an end in itself; it's a preparation for training the mind. Now you can see why. You are no longer just training the senses; you are well on your way to having trained your very capacity for giving attention too. And in the process, you have begun to train the will, far beneath the conscious level.

It can be terribly painful when we see ourselves mastered by some enormous desire or compulsive attachment. We think maybe we'll never get free – think we don't have any will at all. But I always tell my friends, when they confide these feelings to me, that the will is there the whole time, only it's being carried along in the desire itself – like a baby kangaroo, riding in its mother's pouch. It's a whimsical image, but it suggests that the baby won't always stay in the pouch. One day it will heave itself out and hop away on its own strong feet.

. . . that being inwardly cured . . .

Medical scientists have achieved almost miraculous results in learning how to transplant parts of the human body. I would never deprecate their achievements, but I would point out how much more wonderful it would be to get a new mind – a mind that is always at peace, full of love and energy, always ready to work for others. This is what meditation can give us. The great Catholic teacher Hugh of St. Victor described his experience: "I am suddenly renewed: I am changed. I am plunged into an ineffable peace. My mind is full of gladness; all my past wretchedness and pain is forgot. My soul exults, my intellect is illuminated, my heart is afire: my desires have become kindly and gentle."

Indeed, this new mind brings with it enormous bene-fits to health. As meditation deepens and sense cravings fall away, you come to identify yourself less and less with the body. You develop a certain sense of detach-ment, without which it isn't possible to understand the language of the body. You can read its requests accu-rately now, and you'll be impressed to discover that the body has a native wisdom. Fresh, whole, natural food tastes *good* to the palate when the mind is not confusing it with messages planted by advertisers. Vigorous exer-cise feels *good* when the mind whispers to the body: "You were meant for motion!"

. . . and thoroughly cleansed . . .

Layer upon layer, long years of conditioning have over-laid our minds, dulling the bright glow of awareness that is our birthright. Through meditation, these layers of dust and grime are removed. Saint Catherine of

Genoa has described this cleansing process with a beautiful simile:

> It is as with a covered object – it cannot respond to the rays of the sun, not because the sun ceases to shine, for it shines without intermission, but because the covering intervenes. Let the covering be removed and again the object will be exposed to the sun and will answer to the rays which beat against it in proportion as the work of removal advances.

When you meditate on a beautiful passage like the Twenty-third Psalm and take it into the depths of consciousness, it gradually washes clean the very walls of consciousness. It paints them anew with glowing pictures of the human being in the divine image. When you give your complete attention to the Prayer of Saint Francis, you are cleansing your mind. When the great stream of love from the twelfth chapter of the Bhagavad Gita pours into your mind, you are purifying the contents of your mind. The more inspiring the passage and the deeper it goes, the purer your mind becomes. Finally, after many years of meditation, negative thoughts will not be able to enter your mind – the atmosphere just won't sustain them.

. . . I may be made fit to love . . .

When I visit San Francisco I like to go with friends to the Marina, where we can walk for a mile or so right next to the bay. On all sides people are jogging and sprinting, while the sea gulls and pigeons scatter out of their way; and at regular intervals there are exercise stations where some are trying to strengthen their backs, others to strengthen their calf muscles or their thighs. It reminds me of my high school in Kerala, where body-building was highly regarded, and one of the most popular ways to show how strong you were was "making the frog leap" in your biceps.

I'm impressed by how many people are joining health clubs now, and by how much enthusiasm they have for strengthening the body. My suggestion is only this: Why not learn the exercises that will strengthen your mind as well? Where the muscles of patience are weak, as they are with most people today, one little provocation and you are ready to retaliate. You can strengthen those muscles immeasurably through meditation, so that while you don't lose your sensitivity, you become, as the Bible says beautifully, "slow to wrath."

No one at the Marina, and none of the trainers at your workout club, will ever give you special exercises meant to *weaken* particular muscles. But spiritual teachers do this. They help you strengthen your will and patience, but they also say, "Let's see if we can't make those resentment muscles a bit flabby." Do what they say, and before you know it the muscles of resentment and hostility will just lie there. The frogs won't leap at all now, and you will be incapable of hostility.

These are secrets that aren't known in our modern civilization. But they are spelled out succinctly in the Prayer of Saint Francis of Assisi. Meditate on the prayer with the same regularity you give to your morning push-ups or jogging or swimming, and your mind will undergo so dramatic a change that you'll wish you could have "before" and "after" photographs for the newspapers.

As compulsive patterns of living fall away, all the vital energy that has sustained them will come back to you. You really *are* stronger now. And as compulsive attachments fall away, you become capable of slowly extending your love to more and more people. You have more and richer relationships now, and you are increasingly aware that beneath all the teeming diversity of life there is unity. Your arms are strong now. You have a long reach, and it seems like lifetimes ago that you might have described yourself as "weak in love."

The source of your newfound strength, and the keystone of the mystics' Spiritual Fitness Program, is the deceptively simple discipline that characterizes the form of meditation I teach: that is, the training of attention. I ask my students to give their complete attention to the words of the spiritual passage. I ask, too, that *when their attention wanders away from the passage,* as it will, *they should bring it back, gently but firmly.* I tell them to keep doing this over and over, thirty times in thirty minutes if need be.

I promise them that if they do this, they will develop a tremendous skill. When the mind is accustomed to wandering wherever it likes, there can be serious consequences. But see what happens when you have brought it under some control. Now when your attention begins to wander from Rosalind to Celia – as it well might! – you can bring it back to your sweetheart.

Even if Rosalind has had a bad day and is taking it out on you, you can guard your love against going astray and win her undying loyalty in the process.

The wandering mind is one of the frailties of human nature. When our dear one provokes us, we say, "I wish he'd go away." We're all like that. When our beloved is self-willed and won't give us our way, we think, "Why do I have to be with her?" It is this kind of thought, repeated a thousand times, that leads finally to the tragic parting of the ways that we see all around us. And it is the capacity to *break* that train of thought, right at the outset, that makes us "fit to love." As Shakespeare says:

> Love is not love
> That alters when it alteration finds,
> Or bends with the remover to remove.

. . . courageous to suffer . . .

The modern attempt to pretend that life can be all jubilee and merrymaking is futile. We can't conceal the sorrow that throbs at the very heart of life, and it is this sorrow which provides us the means of spiritual growth.

It is a universal law of life, enshrined at the core of every great religion, that when we go after personal satisfaction it will elude us. Read the life of Saint Augustine or Saint Teresa, or of any of the other great lovers of God who have burned their fingers and made their hearts weary before they finally turned inward to find the supreme source from which all truth, joy, and

beauty flow. This inward turning rarely takes place all
at once; for most of us it is long and drawn out. Yet
gently, over many years as our meditation deepens, we
are forced to see the emptiness of what we've clung to –
and indeed very often the things we've clung to break in
our grasp and fall to pieces. It is a terribly painful process, and that is why Saint John of the Ladder says,
"Prayer is the mother and also the daughter of tears."
We grieve at what is slipping away from us, but we
know there is even greater grief in holding on.

Training the senses can be very painful. So is every
skirmish and every battle we undertake against self-
will. At the outset, it can feel – this is no exaggeration –
that something in us is dying, and dying by slow, painful degrees. Yet even as this is taking place, our experience begins to verify the beautiful and mysterious
words of the fourteenth-century German mystic John
Tauler. "In the truest death of all created things," he observed, "the sweetest and most natural life is hidden. In
their death lies the secret of our life." This is not our
world, he is saying. This world of created things is not
the one we were born to inhabit. To find the world that
is our own, the City of God, we must gently, gradually,
but resolutely withdraw our attachment from the world
of physical things.

Tauler continues: "This dying has many degrees. A
person might die a thousand deaths in one day and find
at once a joyful life corresponding to each of them." He
is a subtle psychologist. Suppose you have a strong desire to eat something you have been conditioned to
enjoy for many years. You are able to forget it for a little
while, but then it comes up again. You focus more

intently upon the work at hand, you repeat your mantram, and indeed the desire recedes for a while . . . but then, without warning, up it comes again. It's an exhilarating struggle, because even though you may not be able to erase the urge altogether, every time you manage to set it aside, you get a little more strength with which to fight, a little more vitality. You begin to taste "a joyful life" that indeed corresponds to the death of every selfish urge.

Tauler concludes magnificently by saying, "This is as it must be. God cannot deny or refuse this death. The stronger the death, the more powerful and thorough is the corresponding life. The more intimate the death, the more inward is the life. Each life brings strength, and strengthens to a harder death . . . a death so long and strong that it seems to him hereafter more joyful, for he finds life in death and light shining in darkness." The mind becomes still, the heart becomes full of love, and as a result the body glows and creative faculties come into play. People are drawn to you, and you become a shining lamp to all those who are around.

. . . steady to persevere.

Imposing spiritual disciplines on yourself takes tremendous courage, because it asks you to come face to face with all that is resistant and rebellious inside you. This journey into the world within is real travel, and you'll meet with quite a few unexpected adventures.

The depths of consciousness is an immense region with many levels. On every level of consciousness there is a breathtakingly different view of life, so that when you change levels you have great difficulties. It's very much like going to China: you don't know the language; you don't know the customs; you don't even know how to use chopsticks. Just so, it takes a lot of effort and experience to learn how to operate on a new level of consciousness, where the race-old sense of separateness is beginning to give way to unity. And just when you begin to feel at home in this new region, meditation deepens again, and you enter still another level of consciousness. You've just got used to China and now you're in India. You don't know how to drape a sari or put your hair in a chignon or place a little *tilak* on your forehead – but you learn.

Living on the surface level of consciousness, we do not even know there *is* a world within – a world, what's more, with its own meteorological events. We know, of course, that here in North America we are subject to strong winds – cold ones that bring in a wintry breath from the north, or warm ones like the chinook that come across the Rockies in spring. But we know nothing about the winds that blow inside. People just don't know how to cope with the winds that blow through the mind. Where there is a hot wind, they lose their temper; when it is a cold wind, they get icy; when it's neither hot nor cold, they get bored and do ridiculous things!

With deepening meditation, you realize that when these strong winds come up, you have a choice. You don't have to bend whichever way the wind is blowing.

You don't have to identify with the angry or fearful motions of the mind. Just as wind power can be harnessed, the wind of anger can be harnessed. Gandhi showed us how. The wind of greed can be harnessed, too. Francis of Assisi showed us how.

While modern civilization has made great strides in understanding the external world, it has sadly neglected exploring the internal world. Yet we live in the world within every bit as much as in the world outside. The forces of anger are great hurricanes which can destroy us and others. The forces of greed are gales that can devastate the mind. Fear is a fierce blizzard that can become a terrible burden on the human being. We need to know how these winds blow, and how they can be directed and put to work.

Whenever I see windmills on the hills around us, I am reminded that the powerful winds that sweep our region have been put to work. Similarly, "anger mills" can be set up in consciousness: we can put anger to work. When the destructive winds of anger blow, we can repeat the Holy Name, calm our mind, and turn that rising anger into compassion. Anger is raw power, power that we usually allow to dissipate in meaningless explosions. But we can learn to use anger as a motivation, as Gandhi did when he channeled his anger into nonviolent resistance. Anger, fear, and greed are all powerful forces that can help us, when transformed, to persevere on the spiritual journey. Once we have harnessed their power, they will push us forward rather than hold us back.

In the practice of meditation, what we really learn to do is to discover the world within, which is as real as the world without. I am not denying the reality of mountains, seas, rivers, or forests. But I am also at home in the world within, in which there are tremendous mountains where you can climb to the summit, look about, and exclaim with Angela of Foligno, "The world is full of God!"

Chapter Four

Love is a great thing, yea, a great and thorough good; by itself it makes every thing that is heavy light, and it bears evenly all that is uneven. For it carries a burden which is no burden, and makes every thing that is bitter sweet and tasteful.

Unselfish love is a precious thing, and like all precious things it must be worked for. Our image of the lover may be the young man in a tuxedo dancing cheek to cheek with his sweetheart, but the reality is more like a miner digging in a deep pit for gold or for precious gems. It is hard work, and we have to dig through a lot of ordinary earth before getting anywhere near a diamond or a nugget of gold.

Many years ago, when I was a student, I was traveling with a friend by train when we passed a world-famous gold mine not too many miles from Bangalore and decided to get down and take a look. The mine was run by a British company in a place called the Kolar gold fields. Kolar is located on the vast plains of South India, so when we got out of the train I was surprised to see several huge hills. I told my friend I hadn't known there were hills like that in the area. He knew more about mines than I did, so he just laughed. All the dirt and rock that had covered the hidden gold had been removed, he explained, and there was so much of it that it had become these hills.

I remembered that dramatic terrain when the newspapers were full of the discovery in South Africa of the world's second largest diamond. Weighing in at six hundred carats, it was going to be sold for thirty million dollars. I couldn't read the accounts without trying to recall what the world's *first* largest diamond was. How much did *it* weigh? A friend who is a reference librarian helped me out: it is the Star of Africa, discovered in 1905. It weighed one and one-quarter pounds before it was cut, and it resides now in the Tower of London, where it adorns the British royal scepter.

Of course, if you were to ask the great mystics of East and West, "What is the world's most precious jewel, and where is it?" they would have a very different answer from the *Guinness Book of World Records.* Jesus called it "a pearl of great price." Teresa of Avila says that the human soul "can best be compared to a mansion made of a single diamond," which the Compassionate Buddha refers to in his beautiful mantram *Om mani padme hum:* literally, "The jewel is in the lotus." Every one of us is the possessor of the most precious diamond in the world: it is hidden in the lotus of the heart, in the very depths of consciousness. To get it, we don't have to attend a sale at Christie's or Sotheby's; we have only to claim our legacy. It is always with us; it will always be with us.

The problem is, we don't know this. It is as if we had a hidden treasure in a safe-deposit box. To get the key to that box and claim the treasure, there is a certain price. Thirty million dollars is not enough. Thirty *billion* is not enough. Money counts for nothing in this divine marketplace; but "sweat equity" is precious. We must go deep into consciousness through the practice of meditation, and in order to do that, we must first remove tons and tons of self-will. We have to dig and dig and keep digging. If, at the end of our spiritual journey, we could see all our self-will piled up against the sky, we would be stunned.

I have always been a hardworking person, but I had no idea what unending labor meditation would exact. Almost no one can fathom this. It seems so simple at the outset that people just can't believe it's going to be difficult. "How could sitting still for thirty minutes and concentrating on the soothing words of Saint Francis be a problem?" they ask.

So they begin to sit with me in meditation, and after a month or so, when I ask how their meditation is going, they answer, "Oh, I don't find it so very difficult. Maybe I have a natural aptitude for it!"

I'm not one to throw cold water on natural aptitudes. Who knows, maybe this is one of those one-in-a-million you read about! But once a person breaks through the surface level of consciousness and begins to enter deeper levels, the story changes. Then when I say, "Your meditation must still be going very well?" there is only silence at first, and a pained look.

"Not exactly," comes the reply at last. "I don't know where I'm going any more, and when I try to meditate on the Prayer of Saint Francis, all kinds of thoughts rush in – from restaurants and swimming pools and movie theaters and dental chairs. They come and sit by my side in meditation, and I just don't know what to do."

In feigned innocence I ask, "Why don't you just tell them to go away?"

"I've tried. They just laugh at me!"

At this point, when they have all but despaired, I tell them they are actually doing much better than they think.

"Up until now," I explain, "the ego hasn't taken your efforts seriously, but now it does. Now it is beginning to feel threatened, so it is loosing all its weapons against you: distractions of every kind, and worst of all, the idea 'Oh, who am I, with all my weaknesses and wayward desires, to think I could ever follow this path to the end?' This is no time to get discouraged. Just give your attention more and more to the spiritual passage, and ransack your day for hidden opportunities to go against self-will. A little opportunity here, another there – you will see how your meditation deepens."

I add, too, that we have only to read the lives of people like Augustine and Teresa of Avila to make an enormously comforting discovery: all of these people began with imperfections, just as we do. "Look at that slag pile of self-will!" Augustine would say. "Almost touches the sky, and I had to take out every shovelful by hand! If I can commit all those mistakes and still discover this flawless diamond, don't weep over the mistakes you have committed. Turn your back upon them and start digging!"

By itself it makes everything that is heavy light . . .

What you are removing with pick and shovel in meditation is nothing more than the will to have your own way, solidified in a thousand petty little insistences: "I must have this to drink and that to eat. I must have this kind of music to listen to and that sort of sweater to wear. I won't tolerate people who disagree with my views on contemporary art, and I will avoid the company of anyone who is richer or poorer, older or younger, darker or lighter, brighter or slower, than I am."

The cumulative weight of all these stipulations is tremendous, and much of the sorrow we experience in life has to do with our having to carry it all around. A fourteenth-century spiritual classic, the *Theologia Germanica*, says, "Nothing burns in hell but self-will." We can paraphrase aptly: "Nothing oppresses us in *life* except self-will."

The surest sign of grace, then – and it can come like a bolt out of the blue – is the desire to go against all selfish desires. Mechthild of Magdeburg describes the dawning of this desire in a soul that is just turning inward: "First, that it wills to come to God, removing all self-will, joyfully welcoming God's grace and willingly accepting all its demands against selfish desires."

To take on self-will is a joint endeavor of immense cooperation between divine grace and human effort. It's like a matching grant: the harder we try, the more abundantly grace pours forth from within to augment our effort.

You begin, then, in little, little ways, and at first the whole business seems almost laughable. You order tortellini for dinner when you really wanted fettuccine. You ask for mineral water instead of Chianti, and fresh fruit to round everything off just as your eyes start to slide toward the dessert list. This is hardly the stuff that hair shirts are made of, but you *are* reducing self-will, and you do notice a certain alertness entering your life and a new mettle. Part of your mind leaps out, "But I'd *so* looked forward to that fettuccine." But another part now replies, "Oh, hush! Pasta's pasta." You are in the driver's seat now, in a way that can feel quite pleasurable.

Be warned, though, that progress will be uneven. You can try a more daring raid on self-will the next morning, and find you've tumbled right out of the driver's seat onto the hard pavement. But you brush yourself off and carry on, exhilarated – and keenly interested.

Most of us pay little attention to the movements of our mind over the course of a day. We don't notice how, when there are differences of opinion or when events don't work out as we'd hoped, the mind surges up and down, moves wildly to and fro, and grumbles, "I don't *like* this." But with our new perspective, we almost look forward to life trying to knock us off our pins.

In my own case, for instance, there is a certain very well known newspaper in this country whose editorial page contradicts almost all my views on life. Of course, I could just avoid reading it. Instead, for years I have gone out of my way to read it every day. I have actually taught myself to enjoy reading articles about the supreme importance of money. "So, it seems the measure of a nation's strength is its gross national product. Hmmm." There is no question in my mind but that I disagree. Yet my mind, as I read, is unperturbed. It makes no convulsive movements. In fact, it almost chuckles. I am able to read attentively and follow thoroughly the line of thinking.

Similarly, on evenings when I want to entertain myself with a good book, my inclination in the past would have been to pull a volume of Robert Browning's poetry off the shelf, or a play by George Bernard Shaw. Instead, I now reach for a stack of medical journals. The articles are seldom well-written; often they are even badly edited. But I read them in order to keep abreast of medical goings-on – and because of my deep interest in the connection between meditation and health, I read not in protest but with gusto. Medieval mystics mortified the flesh; I have mortified my literary sensibilities.

Once you have lost the dread of being contradicted, or even of being disappointed aesthetically, a kind of inward cheerfulness pervades your mind. You find that you think more clearly under duress, your blood pressure unaffected. You wear your opinions more loosely, carry your self-will more lightly; so you function better in life.

Tragically, when self-will is highly developed, it has the effect of narrowing our vision of life down to a tiny peephole. When we're only thinking of what's in our immediate personal interest, we just don't see things clearly. We can't take in the larger picture. If we did, we'd see that our own welfare is neatly interlocked with everyone else's – that separateness is the illusion born of preoccupation with self. There is no more ideal place to begin breaking free from that preoccupation than in the company of our family and friends. In today's world where so many people, whether through necessity or through choice, plough a lonely furrow, we need to be reminded of the importance of living and working with other people – building strong, selfless, loving relationships wherever possible.

It is love that teaches us our real stature and reveals the heroism we never thought we possessed. The small renunciation that might be well-nigh impossible in a vacuum can be blessedly simple when someone we love stands to gain. This is surely part of what Thomas a Kempis means when he says that love makes everything that is heavy light. Turning down that glass of Chianti might take some doing in ordinary circumstances, but when you're in the company of an impressionable teenager, you'll gladly set it aside. Or suppose you're tempted to add another antique fire screen to your collection. Hard to resist, maybe, if your aim is solely to reduce your own self-will. But if the money you save can be spent on a tent for family camping trips – something everybody can enjoy – then saying no to the temptation can be a breeze. You feel so good inside! A knack for quiet self-sacrifice is the very life and soul of family living.

The annals of ancient monastic communities, East or West, relate how in a thousand ways members would go after self-will in acts of fierce deprivation, such as sleeping without lying down, or eating only one meal a day for years on end. This approach might have had its merits; but my way is, I think, subtler, and much better suited to the world of today. Each of us can find ways to simplify our lives and reduce our needs – what we eat, what we wear, how much we drive, how we spend our leisure time. All the daily choices we make can work to reduce self-will. They can also take into account our endangered environment and all the living creatures that inhabit it. Reducing self-will needn't be a joyless exercise. It can be achieved through many little acts of love, performed over and over throughout the day.

We start, then, by recognizing that the sense of *I* and *mine* we've cultivated all our lives is like a coil wrapped tight around our necks, throttling us, and that the more we dwell on ourselves, the tighter it gets. Gradually, we now start extending our concern more and more to the people immediately around us, by learning to see that their needs are just as urgent as our own. As the coil loosens, we can breathe more easily. The coil is still there, but the distinction between our families' needs and our own has begun to dissolve.

This is no place to stop. It is time to enlarge the circle of attention and compassion still further. You might forgo an evening at the theater to attend a town council, because there needs to be a community center for the aged and better parks for the children. Little by little, in loving gestures, you stretch the confines of self-will outward. You are not obliterating the old nagging *I* and *mine* by a frontal attack. Rather, you are extending your boundaries outward until they include all of life. In the words of Catherine of Genoa, "Everything is mine, for all that is God's seems to be wholly mine. I am mute and lost in God."

Not that this comes easily. I did not find it the least bit enjoyable to forgo some of my earlier pleasures. But when you want this more than anything else, when you want *God* – not intellectually, not theoretically, but with all your heart, all your mind, and all your spirit – then you get the will, the wisdom, and the courage to give up whatever stands in the way. That "whatever" may be extremely pleasant, and you may have been conditioned to it for a long time. But if you want the Lord passionately enough, you will succeed in letting go.

. . . and it bears evenly all that is uneven.

Whenever I hear someone say "I got even with him," I want to point out, "But you didn't! You got odd – odder and odder." When we can't let go of our anger, when we allow it to push us about and damage our relationships, we lose something of our essential humanity. The artists of medieval Europe used to portray anger, envy, and greed as monsters with bared fangs and terrible horns. The contemporary teenager who describes his aggravated father as "bent out of shape" is getting at the same truth in his own wry idiom.

The ability to forgive is the hallmark of the highly evolved human being. There is no more exacting skill.

And yet it is nothing more, essentially, than the seemingly prosaic capacity of withdrawing attention at will and placing it where you choose. Whatever distressing words have been spoken, whatever unkind acts have been performed, the mind that has been trained in deep meditation can turn quietly away and focus instead on the loving words, the thoughtful acts, of a happier hour.

Like any skill, this one develops with practice. Suppose you are meditating on the words of Thomas a Kempis: "Love bears evenly all that is uneven." Suddenly a much louder passage is ringing in your ears. It is as if a car with huge speakers had pulled up next to yours at a stoplight, playing a tape of something someone has said to you that day: "Charles, I think it's time both of us started seeing other people!" or "Marilou, you're just not working out as an administrator. I've decided you'd be more effective back in your old post."

The more attention you give to these dissonant voices, the louder they'll get. The only way to turn them down is to give your attention more and more to the words of the passage: "Love bears evenly all that is uneven." It is a simple skill, but it has wide applications. When you have a severe personal problem, you are naturally inclined to dwell on it, and when you do, it looms all the larger. Solutions seem more and more distant. Most problems are rather unassuming when you see them in their native costume. They only become unmanageable when you can't stop brooding on them, dressing them up as Count Dracula or Lady Macbeth.

When someone who is close to you lashes out over nothing, or lets you down in a way that really grieves you, it is natural that you should find it difficult to have loving thoughts. It is altogether understandable that you should want to move away from that person. But when you have developed the capacity to step back from the turmoil of an offended mind and look at the situation with even a small measure of objectivity, you can make a fascinating discovery. Often the person who is causing us trouble is simply making a call for help – calling in the only language he or she knows. Underneath the abrasiveness is a hidden message: "Please move closer to me. Support me. Bear with me."

We all know how much turmoil there is in living together. This is why so many follow the counsel of despair and say, "Why not live by ourselves? Why be unhappy?" But for ordinary people like you and me, the solitary life is not particularly conducive to spiritual growth. To purify our hearts of self-will no amount of reading books can be of much help; no amount of discussion will do the job. Seminars on Self-Will Extinction are beside the point. There is only one way to undo self-will, and that is by living and working harmoniously with other people. In the sometimes painful give-and-take of life every day, you can draw upon the power released in meditation to love and support the people around you – even at the expense of your own comfort and convenience.

The mystics are unanimous: love of God makes itself seen and felt as love of our fellow creatures. Only when you have lowered all the barriers between yourself and others will there be no barrier between you and the Lord within. Deliberately, then, from the very first, you begin to chip away at those walls in consciousness. You do it in little ways, throughout the day, by trying to see the needs of others as clearly as your own and to act in harmony with them.

Another discipline that comes very naturally into the picture at this point is spiritual fellowship, spending time with others who meditate, who share your ideals and your efforts to realize them. The support you can provide one another will strengthen your meditation enormously. Don't confine yourself to fellow aspirants of your own time and place. Your stoutest spiritual allies may have lived ten or twenty centuries ago – Saint Teresa of Avila or the Compassionate Buddha, John Woolman or Saint Catherine of Genoa. Daily reading from the scriptures and from the lives of the great mystics is a richly rewarding side of the spiritual life.

It carries a burden which is no burden . . .

On our village roads in Kerala, people carry all kinds of things on their heads. Whether they are bringing water jugs from the well, or carrying butter and yogurt to the market place, or taking baskets of laundry down to the river, everything goes on the head. This is wisdom born of experience, because it is best for the back and makes for beautiful posture.

Even so, the loads are heavy, and after a while the back begins to weary. So at intervals along our footpaths and country roads there are stone pillars called *athanis*, just the height of a man or woman. They are flat on top so that you can slide your burden off and rest for a moment. When the day is warm and you have a mile or two to travel, nothing could be more welcome than the sight of one of these pillars just ahead.

The *athani* is a humble, ordinary feature of the Kerala landscape. But it makes a glorious appearance in a tender poem written by a Kerala poet about Mary Magdalene. The poet himself was a devout Hindu, but he was so moved when he heard the story of Mary Magdalene that he retold it in Malayalam, my native tongue. He chose a particularly soft and gentle meter, to tell the Gospel story in his own Kerala way.

Mary Magdalene is described as a deeply troubled person whom the whole village looked down on for her dissolute life – someone who had despaired, in all likelihood, of ever being able to put her past behind her. When she heard that Jesus was nearby, she slipped in behind him while he was at dinner, fell to her knees, and began to weep. She washed his feet with her tears and dried them with her long, lustrous hair, because she knew that here was somebody who was incapable of sitting in judgment on her.

"Weep, lovely one, weep!" says the Lord. "Let all your suffering pour out." He knows her tears are easing a heart that has been ready to break under the weight of her grief. "You who have eyes like a doe's, your eyes are even more beautiful now when you wash away the past. Let those same tears purify your mind as well." Then he makes her a tender promise. "I will be your *athani*. Just hand over the burden of your past. My arms are strong; I can carry it all." And he adds gently, "Your sins are forgiven. Go in peace."

In the Hindu tradition, one of the names of the Lord is "the ocean of forgiveness." If we want to be united with him, we need to forgive all those around us, for in learning to forgive we move closer and closer to the Lord, who is the source of forgiveness itself.

When you begin to travel inward through meditation you will see for yourself how many things the mind has not been able to pardon. For a while, all you can do is look at them in dismay. But if over many years you have developed compassion for others, then that same wealth of compassion will come to you when you most need it. It will equip you with a kind of spiritual eraser. Now you will be able to walk up to a memory that has spread hostility, fear, or greed in your mind for decades and just rub it out.

If anyone were to ask me about the mistakes I made in the past, I would say simply, "That was how I saw life then. Now, through the grace of the Lord, my vision has been corrected." That is why I repeat over and over again, "Don't let your mind dwell on the past." Everybody has scars from the past. Don't talk about them; don't think about them. I am the first to admit that this is a tall order. It can be done, though, through repetition of the Holy Name.

*. . . and makes everything that is bitter
sweet and tasteful.*

Saint Bernard declared that "Jesus is honey in the
mouth, music in the ear, a shout of gladness in the
heart." Saint Bernard very probably repeated the name
of Jesus to himself just as good Hindus do the name of
Rama or Krishna. Saint Catherine of Genoa may have
engaged in the same practice, for at the time of her conversion she is said to have received certain instructions
directly from the Lord within. "From the 'Hail Mary,'"
she was told, "take the word *Jesus,* and may it be im-
planted in your heart, and it will be a sweet guide and
shield to you in all the necessities of life." When she was
comforting the patients in the hospital she administered
in Genoa, she would always urge them to "call Jesus."
Biographers of Saint Francis of Assisi describe him as
praying all night on occasion, repeating the same words
over and over: "My God and my all, my God and my
all." And in the Eastern Orthodox tradition, the practice called *hesychasm* consists in the repetition of the
short prayer "Lord Jesus Christ, have mercy upon
me."

Repetition of the Holy Name is not a substitute for
meditation. When you meditate, you need to sit down
in a quiet place with your eyes closed and bring your attention to rest on the words of a memorized passage.
The Holy Name, I want to emphasize, can be used
under *any* circumstances. You can use it throughout the
day to tap into the peace and security of your morning's
meditation. It can be your lifeline. The more assidu-

ously you repeat it, the stronger the rope will be, and the closer at hand in times of danger.

The most precious period of the day for repeating your mantram is at night, just as you are falling asleep. Between the last waking moment and the first sleeping moment, there is an infinitesimally narrow tunnel into the unconscious. If you can learn to fall asleep in the Holy Name, you can send it in deep where it will heal the wounds the day has inflicted; it will soothe the raw edges of daily experience. The proof that the Holy Name is doing its work is that sometimes you may hear it reverberating in your sleep.

This is the miracle Saint Paul refers to when he enjoins us to "pray without ceasing." It goes on wherever you are, whatever you are doing, protecting your mind against any negative emotion. In fact, I like to compare the Holy Name to a highway patrolman riding about on a Harley-Davidson, round and round the alleys of the mind – most of them blind. He keeps an eye on the thoughts traveling there and gives out tickets for excessive speed, for drifting back and forth across lanes, for driving too close to the car ahead. Day and night, your mantram is always on duty.

Chapter Five

The noble love of Jesus impels a man to do great things, and stirs him up to be always longing for what is more perfect.

Love desires to be aloft, and will not be kept back by any thing low and mean.

Love desires to be free, and estranged from all worldly affections, that so its inward sight may not be hindered; that it may not be entangled by any temporal prosperity, or by any adversity subdued.

These lyrical lines convey a feeling of tension between the sheer weight of ordinary life – its disappointments, its cares, its bitterness – and the longing to soar upward, free from any hindrance or entanglement. This tension hints in turn at a deeper one: between the things of this world, as Saint Teresa termed them, and the things of heaven. Clinging to the world kept her bound for nearly forty years; a deep surge of longing for higher things enabled her at last to break free.

Teresa's friend John of the Cross described this dilemma – which is the dilemma of every one of us – in a treatise on the spiritual life called *The Ascent of Mount*

Carmel. The work is prefaced by a rough sketch of a mountain crisscrossed by paths. At the top of the mountain is Earthly Paradise – not heaven but heaven on earth, life as it is meant to be lived. At the bottom of the mountain you see the beginnings of two routes. One is wide and inviting; the other is small and narrow, curving about tortuously among rocky crevasses. The choice seems obvious at first glance. But as your eye travels upward, you see that the path that had seemed so attractive begins to coil back upon itself. It shrinks in size, and finally vanishes in the thick undergrowth of the lower slopes. This is the path of least resistance, of saying "Yes, of course!" to every murmur from the senses and the ego.

The other path, so hard at the outset, becomes gradually wider and easier of access as it ascends, and it carries you with increasing ease and delight all the way to the top. This is the path of spiritual discipline. The difference is this: on the one hand, a life ruled by self-will, and on the other, one that is lived for the whole.

The noble love of Jesus impels a man to do great things, and stirs him up to be always longing for what is more perfect.

During the Winter Olympics that were held at Calgary in 1988, everyone was impressed by a champion ski-jumper they called the Flying Finn, who was able to soar through the air for seventy meters. He looked like an eagle – head thrust forward, wings folded back. To my inexperienced eye, what he was doing looked absolutely impossible. But when I consulted friends who ski, they said, "No, it's not impossible. But it takes a tremendous lot of training." Most of the greatest ski-jumpers have practiced since childhood. Matti Nykanen, it is said, was so enraptured by skiing – the dangers so beckoned to him – that he jumped off a roof when he was only seven. It was to protect him from serious injury that his parents gave him a pair of skis and set him loose on the slopes. He was asked, "How many times do you jump on your skis?" His answer: four to five thousand times a year – which is nearly ten times a day.

Watching Matti Nykanen on television, amazed by his ability, I thought of the words of the medieval German mystic who prefaced his treatise with a warning: if you don't like challenges, he said, don't read this book. My guess is that with that warning he attracted exactly the reckless young aspirants he was after – the Matti Nykanens of the spiritual life – because the best and brightest young people *want* difficult things to do. They don't want us to mince words; they don't want us to coat the pill. They want tremendous challenges to pit themselves against. Meditation is the hardest path the human being can walk on; but when I tell my young friends outright how grueling the later stages of meditation can be, their faces glow at the prospect.

It's a great pity that the roiling turbulence of young men and women is so often seen as a threat to society. Rightly understood and channeled, that restlessness can be the most precious asset of any society, because it arises directly out of the need that is deepest in every human being: the need to give. It is when that need is blocked that the trouble starts, and grievously enough, the trouble often comes in the form of self-destructive behavior.

Many young people in this country have satisfied their physical appetites over and over. Now they yearn for a higher goal. It is as if there has been an opening from inside out of which tremendous yearning, tremendous energy, comes up. It is so powerful and demanding that young people have got to find some way of putting it to work. Misunderstanding it, they do the most dangerous and meaningless things possible. The real answer is not to chastise them or be punitive, but to show them through our own example what this tremendous energy is meant for – and that the more it is utilized, the more they will get from within. It's a wonderful discovery for a young person to make: that beneath all these drives to rebel there flows this deep desire to give and to serve.

The wealth of a country does not lie in mines, factories, or shopping centers; it lies in the hearts of young people. My grandmother understood this implicitly, simple village woman though she was. Very often, living in an orthodox Hindu society, I would question some of its assumptions and try to go against them. I had all the makings of a successful rebel. But I never got an opportunity to make much of a splash because my grandmother would usually support me, even though she observed all the orthodox ways herself.

Sometimes, I have to confess, this was rather deflating. Confronted by my latest effort to challenge the time-honored ways of my village, she would only say, "The capacity to rebel is part of our human wealth. It is God-given." When the Lord is making a human being, she would explain, he takes a good measure of rebelliousness and mixes it in. He has his reasons. Rebelliousness is given to us so that in time, once we come to understand ourselves and life, we will use it to rebel against all that is selfish, base, and separate in ourselves.

Unfortunately, most of us never get that far. Not knowing what all that energy is for, we use it to rebel against parents, partner, community – whoever is around. When the time comes to rebel against ourselves, we've used up all the fuel.

When Thomas uses the phrase "the noble love of Jesus," he is describing the burning idealism that can propel a young man or woman into acts of great courage and self-sacrifice. You can see, then, how tragically we betray our young people when we hold out for them as goals a good pension plan, a rapid promotion ladder, a home in one of the best neighborhoods. Today's epidemic of suicide among children and teenagers has to do directly with this betrayal. They urgently need a sense of direction, and there is only one way to provide it: for us to transform ourselves. We need to show them, by our own example, how impatience and restlessness can be used.

It is no coincidence that whenever someone sets out to live selflessly in response to this "noble love" of God, young people gravitate to that person in large numbers. When Mother Teresa left her teaching position in Calcutta to serve the city's poor, the young women who had been her students couldn't wait to join her work.

When Mahatma Gandhi set out to free India, my country's young people pressed forward from all sides. These towering individuals had what young people are always looking for: a cause to which they can devote their lives.

Love desires to be aloft, and will not be
kept back by any thing low and mean.

I have already mentioned the great teacher from the Eastern Orthodox tradition known as John of the Ladder. The name suggests a fascinating picture. You can imagine John taking his ladder everywhere, so that he can climb step by step to the highest peak of consciousness. When you are practicing meditation and following the allied disciplines, you are climbing that same ladder. You can call yourself Stuart of the Ladder, Sarah of the Ladder; and this ladder is the very best gift you can give your children. When you want to teach children how to use a stepladder, you don't lecture them; you just set it up right there in the living room. In a spiritual home, the parents set up John's ladder and show how it is to be climbed. And as the children watch, they will be climbing too; they will grow in understanding, patience, and selflessness.

In each one of us there is an upward urge – a deep inner voice that asks us to continue to evolve, growing taller day by day, until we attain our full height. But there is also another voice, loud and raucous, which keeps saying, "Remain stunted; stay selfish; stay sensuous." This is the "low and mean" side of consciousness. The spiritual life can be characterized as the long drawn-out struggle between these two voices. The voice of selfishness seems particularly loud at first, because it is so near at hand – right here at the surface level of consciousness. The other voice is very faint at the outset. But when you go deeper and deeper into consciousness in meditation, you discover gradually that your real needs are not for personal satisfaction. Go after your own satisfaction day and night, for weeks on end, and you will still feel restless and insecure. Once you start taking cues, though, from that other voice – "Be kind; think of others" – the security and peace you'd been looking for begin to fill your life and buoy your spirits. Not only that, as you listen more and more to this new voice, it becomes musical and incomparably beautiful. You don't have to force this; it comes about naturally as meditation deepens. You begin to think as urgently about the needs of others as you've been thinking about your own. All the old heaviness has gone. You feel light – "aloft," in Thomas's own words.

But at the beginning of the spiritual life, when your attention is split between these two urges, it can be very painful. I've told my Californian friends that it is like trying to climb El Capitan in Yosemite. You are burning with desire to make it to the top, only you've carefully put on handcuffs, leg irons, and a tremendous load on your back.

"Rick," the experienced mountaineer might ask, "where are you going?"

"Oh, I'm off to climb El Capitan."

"But what's all this? Leg irons, handcuffs, and a huge backpack?"

"Oh, this?" says Rick proudly. "This is my equipment, developed over a long period."

"You'll find it a lot easier," the more seasoned climber suggests, "if you can free your hands."

Rick blanches. "You mean, give up my gear? Sounds impossible to me."

But his friend persists. "Let's try it anyway."

With trepidation, Rick sets his handcuffs aside and addresses the precipitous granite face.

"Hey!" he shouts. "I can grip better! Raise myself better! I didn't know this."

Now his friend gently suggests that the leg irons could go too. Once more there is a shudder of apprehension, but *clank!* go the leg irons. "Hey!" Rick shouts again. "I have freedom of movement now! My hands are free! My feet are free!"

"Yeah," his friend says, "but you've still got a ridiculous load on your back. Sure, you need water and ropes. Rations for a few days, and a sleeping bag. But all this other junk has got to go." Soon there is a big pile on the ground – all the things Rick doesn't need. And if you look hard at the face of El Capitan you can see Rick moving along at a good clip – almost to the top.

In a sense, *desire* is the single most important word in this passage from *The Imitation of Christ*. Thomas is saying that through the choices we make in everyday life, we can strengthen the desire for spiritual awareness – the upward drive. For example, we can read uplifting books instead of spy thrillers. We can steep ourselves in the lives and writings of the great mystics until they haunt our very sleep. And we can spend time with others who share our desire for spiritual growth.

At the same time, we can *withdraw* our energy and attention from those activities for which the downward impulse clamors. We can stay away from violent and sensate motion pictures. We can forgo our Saturday morning perusal of the mail-order catalogs in order to give the time freely and generously to our family. We can help staff a shelter for homeless families, or volunteer to drive meals to elderly people who are housebound.

Every deep desire is a prayer, whether you spell it out to God or not. Desire is power, and when you have a deep, strong, unified desire, the power of that desire will drive you into action. If that desire is selfless, immense creativity, initiative, and courage will pour into your hands. This great surge *is* the Lord answering your prayer – not from somewhere outside, but from deep within.

The Lord answers every selfless prayer, but the initial unification of desires is up to us. Many people who try meditation complain about their inability to make real progress, even though they have been meditating for some time. I always point out that the driving force that takes us upward is the power of desire, and therefore it is essential to recall desires from wasteful channels. I am not talking about right or wrong now, or moral and immoral. Even a little desire has a lot of power packed in it. We have accumulated a tremendous store of scientific and technological know-how in today's world, but very few of us suspect that it is in our desires that all our power lies. Unfortunately, most of us have no way to get at all this power. The sages tell us that if we can find a way to reach those desires in the depths of our consciousness, we will have the equivalent of a powerful booster rocket. One by one, we can recall our vital energy from sensory cravings and selfish desires and unify it through the practice of meditation into one great, shining, powerful desire that will take us right up into higher consciousness: blast off from Cape Kennedy, right there inside!

The fascinating thing about all this is you aren't always aware that you are dislodging a long-standing compulsive desire until after the fact. You are trying to go deeper in meditation, and the very intensity of your effort pulls energy in from wherever it can. You don't give up smoking; smoking gives you up. You don't give up alcohol; it gives you up. If you go deep enough, where the cravings lie, and are able to withdraw energy from those cravings, those urges cannot trouble you again.

Unfortunately, the conspiracy today is to inflate those desires. Through the talents of the advertisers we are encouraged to indulge them, intensify them. It's for our own protection, then, that we develop the skill of deflating desires. There is nothing more satisfying. Among my own friends, I have watched with delight as addictive desires slowly deflate like so many balloons. You can almost hear the air hissing out. I have been able to anticipate this and say, "In a few weeks' time the balloon is going to be flat. Don't cry. Be glad!"

Love desires to be free, and estranged from all worldly affections . . .

Thomas a Kempis is reminding us that we should not confuse love with compulsive attachment. When the great mystics speak of love, they mean the capacity to see the Lord in every living creature: not just in the immediate family, not just in a sweetheart or best friend. By *love* they mean the capacity to see what is in the best interest of all and act accordingly.

Love that is "estranged from all worldly affections" is not based on physical appearance. It has nothing to do with what this person can do for me or what that person can provide for me. It has only to do with loving the Self within. This kind of love grants perfect freedom. It allows us to act wisely in every situation because it widens our vision, allowing us to see the whole picture. "Love is infallible," said William Law. "It has no errors, for all errors are the want of love."

We should not be discouraged when at the outset we find this kind of love to be impossible. It is a gradual development, which grows as we release ourselves from compulsive desires and come to see that we are not the body.

That so its inward sight may not be hindered . . .

In my beautiful village there were no electric lights when I was a boy. At the end of the school day we would play soccer, and afterwards swim in the cool river. By the time we turned towards home, the shadows of evening would have fallen. Night comes swiftly in the tropics: one minute the sky is glowing with color and then suddenly it's dark. But in those days before electric light, our eyes were so accustomed to the darkness that we could skip along the paths as though it were broad daylight.

Years later, when I had gone away to the university and got used to electric lights, I came back on vacation and found I had lost this knack. I couldn't see in the dark. My friends teased me: "Hey, we thought you were getting *brighter!*"

A long time afterward, while I was living with my mother on the Blue Mountain in South India, I began taking long walks in the evenings. And one night I realized that I was seeing in the dark once again. My night vision had come back.

This experience came to mind years later when I read these striking words from Saint Augustine: "Our whole business in life is to restore to health the eye of the heart, whereby God may be seen." What Thomas a Kempis calls "inward sight" Augustine calls "the eye of the heart." We are all born with this eye, only sheer disuse keeps it closed. When it begins to open we feel as if someone has just given us an extremely high-powered flashlight. Its brilliant light allows us not only to see things but to see *into* them. We no longer see just the external appearance of people; we see into their hearts. This means that when we see somebody who is leading a very troubled life, we can see the circumstances that have made him that way; and we will refrain from judging him.

I have always had a special fondness for the Greek philosopher Plotinus, partly because he wanted to go to India. Like Saint Augustine, he too described an "inward sight." "You must close the eyes," he wrote, "and waken in yourself that other power of vision which is the birthright of all, but which few turn to use." When you waken this new power of vision, he would explain, you will see the One. Every philosopher has his favorite metaphors, and for Plotinus it was always "the One." There may appear to be four billion people on earth, he would say, but there is really only One.

I heard a perfect illustration of Plotinus's doctrine of the One recently when a friend described taking his little boy, Abraham, to the county fair. Abe went into the hall of mirrors and found himself confronted by all kinds of versions of himself: a tall, thin Abe, another Abe who was short and round, a crooked Abe and a wavy one . . . He must have wondered, "Who are all these different people?" But then he recognized his own face in all the variations, and he concluded wisely that no matter how many Abes there appeared to be, in fact there was only one, and it was he. The illusion lay in the manipulation of mirrors.

It is very much the same story with us when we discover our real identity. Afterwards we are never taken in by appearance. George may have a moustache, Tom a beard, and Michael both, but I am not taken in by beards or moustaches. I say, "It's all the One, *appearing* as George, *appearing* as Michael, *appearing* as Tom." This is not just a verbal statement. It is a living knowledge, which enables me to treat all of them with love, no matter what the provocation – and, when I have to oppose them, to do so with tenderness and respect.

That it may not be entangled by any temporal prosperity . . .

One day, the chroniclers tell us, Saint Francis of Assisi whittled a fine cup out of wood, and when it was finished he set it before him on the altar where he carried out his private worship. He looked at it with satisfaction and said to himself, "Francis, that's a nice piece of work, if I do say so."

Then he began to pray, and soon he became deeply absorbed. But after a while, he realized that his attention had drifted back to the cup. "How perfectly the grain of the wood reflects the light! What a lustrous polish!" No sooner did he see that his thoughts had drifted from God than he got to his feet, picked up the cup, and threw it into the fire.

Stories like this are preserved carefully down through the ages because they convey priceless spiritual truths –

in this case, the simple realization that attention can get caught in *any*thing. What I would add is that when attention gets caught, our capacity for loving does too. I have known many people who say they cannot love, whose love was in fact widely distributed among a great multiplicity of objects.

We have been ruthlessly conditioned to think we can find fulfillment in possessions, to love things rather than people – so much so that when we feel an emptiness in our hearts, we go to shopping centers to fill it up. I am all for living in reasonable comfort, but when I go to shopping centers I get alarmed – not so much at the money that is being wasted as at the loss of *will*. No one has enough will to waste, and no one has enough energy to waste. This is the real energy crisis of our civilization: too much of our vitality and drive are being diverted into meeting the demands of personal greed.

When you go deeper into consciousness, you gradually make the discovery that your real needs are not for your own personal satisfaction and aggrandizement. Your real needs are for adding to and enriching the lives of others.

. . . or by any adversity subdued.

In the early stages of meditation, what we are doing is setting the sails of our little boats by training our attention and bringing our senses under control. As Saint Francis de Sales said, "It is not we who make the gale of inspiration blow for us . . . but we simply receive the gale, consent to its motion, and let our ship sail under it, not hindering it by our resistance." We just have to be ready – and part of that readiness is the willingness to travel light. No time now for taking on new attachments; time rather to get rid of most of the ones we already have.

When we drive across the Oakland bridge, I often see big cargo ships resting at anchor, and sometimes I notice that the bottom part of the ship is painted a different color from the upper part. A friend once explained this to me. If the boat is absolutely full, he told me, it's riding so low in the water that you can't see the second color. But when all the cargo has been removed, then it's a two-colored boat again. Most of us, when we undertake the spiritual life, are listing very low in the water, and no one can see the second color at all. This means we have a lot of unloading to do – cargo we may have been accumulating for decades. This unloading doesn't take place overnight. We can't hire a crew of longshoremen with big muscles to do the work for us. We have to unload the boat ourselves; and, worse yet, we really would rather keep most of the cargo. This is where the "adversity" Thomas speaks of comes into our lives.

My sympathies are all with you. I know the unloading doesn't come easily. You seize some heavy attachment and run to the rails with it, and then you feel such a stab of heartache that you carry it all back again.

You may try this over and over – starting to throw out, then changing your mind. And even when you do manage to get rid of some old selfish piece of luggage, there may still be pain and a twinge of regret. But toward the latter part of meditation, when you regain the "inward sight" Thomas speaks of, you begin to catch tantalizing glimpses of the other shore. There is Saint Francis of Assisi with his cowl and rope belt and sandals, and you hear him singing "My God and my all!" There is Saint Teresa, with the castanet and tambourine she played when she and her sisters danced before the Lord. When you glimpse these great spiritual figures in the depths of your meditation, and hear their song, all the longing in your heart bursts forth and you seize every selfish attachment you can lay hands on. At this point there is a danger that you will even throw out the rudder. That is where your spiritual teacher will come to your rescue – grab your arm as you're about to toss and say, "You need that rudder. And that sail! And even a few provisions. Don't get carried away!"

Chapter Six

Nothing is sweeter than love, nothing more courageous, nothing higher, nothing wider, nothing more pleasant, nothing fuller nor better in heaven and earth; because love is born of God, and cannot rest but in God, above all created things.

When Thomas says that "nothing is sweeter than love," he is speaking the language of the experienced world traveler: "I've been everywhere on this globe, friend, and I'm here to tell you there is *nowhere* like Bali." You could substitute "Corfu" or "the Isle of Man," but if your travels, like Thomas's, have taken place deep inside, you will speak as Julian of Norwich did: "I saw the soul, so large as it were an endless world, and also as it were a blessed kingdom . . . a worshipful city."

Until we get into the deeper stages of meditation, we cannot imagine the vast continents that spread across the immensity of consciousness. Millions of thoughts, millions of feelings, millions of urges, drives, hopes, and fears lie just below the surface level. To break through the rocky crust of the ego and enter this other world takes a powerful will and a long period of discipline. But when at last it does open and you slip through, there is a curious feeling in the pit of your stomach. You are entering a world you never thought existed at all. You see a floor that has no bottom, a roof that is endless. You see the bottomless floor of consciousness, the endless roof of consciousness, the boundless space of the *room*. You look out across this vast new world and you wonder, "But how am I to travel here? There is no path, and I don't know where to go!"

In the Hindu tradition, it is said that when a spiritual aspirant sets out on this epic journey, he or she needs two wings: one is discrimination, the other detachment. The words are alliterative in Sanskrit too – *viveka* and *viraga*. Both come with deepening meditation, but it is also true that if we cultivate them in our daily life, meditation will deepen.

It pleased me immensely to find that in a passage which occurs earlier in *The Imitation of Christ*, Thomas a Kempis uses the same compelling imagery: "By two wings a man is lifted up from things earthly, namely, by simplicity and purity. Simplicity ought to be in our intention, purity in our affections. Simplicity doth tend towards God; purity doth apprehend and taste him." It would be hard to define discrimination more aptly than as "simplicity in intention," hard to explain detachment more precisely than as "purity in our affections."

In the vocabulary of Madison Avenue, the man of discrimination is one who knows a fine set of luggage when he sees it. The discriminating woman is one who knows where to buy her cosmetics. Mr. and Ms. Discrimination recognize top quality in any consumer item; shoddy simulations will never take them in. In the vocabulary of mysticism, on the other hand, the measure of our discrimination is how accurately we are able to distinguish between the real and the unreal – between joy that lasts and its fleeting counterfeit, pleasure.

There is a phrase in Sanskrit that characterizes the attitude of the man or woman of discrimination: *neti, neti,* "not this, not this." They look at fame and see that it will not satisfy them. They look at power and know it will never meet their deepest needs. They pass through life very much as a discerning shopper strolls through a department store looking for just the right silk tie. "Not that one," they murmur as their eyes search the racks. "No, that won't do."

When you search tirelessly for the business suit with classic lines, the mystics tell us, it is permanence itself you are after. When you comb the shops for the most exquisite earrings, it is the allure of beauty itself that draws you. So why stay on the periphery of life? Why not go to the source of all permanence and all beauty? Only be warned that when you go on this kind of shopping spree, cost can be no object. You must be willing to stake all you have. Mechthild of Magdeburg said it boldly:

> Wouldst thou come with me to the wine cellar?
> That will cost thee much;
> Even hadst thou a thousand marks
> It were all spent in one hour!
> If thou wouldst drink the unmingled wine,
> Thou must ever spend more than thou hast,
> And the host will never fill thy glass to the brim.

The touchstone against which we are meant to test everything in life is our driving need for joy that is permanent, for "the unmingled wine." To drink from this cup, we are not asked to close our eyes and ears to the beauties of this world – "all created things," in Thomas's words – but we *are* expected to see their limitations. "God has intended us for happiness," says Mechthild, "with greater love than can be imagined." The pleasures of food and drink or other sensory pursuits are genuine enough, but once we have had the tremendous experience of transforming anger into sympathy or ill will into good will, sense pleasures pale into insignificance. Only when we have tasted both kinds of experience can we assess them accurately. When Thomas says that "nothing is sweeter than love," he speaks with the conviction of one who knows that the source of all sweetness is within.

Discrimination is what lets us make wise choices. It brings with it the capacity to see where our choices lead us. It is an insightfulness that grows with use. Each time I choose what will benefit my family or my community over what will bring me a passing, personal satisfaction, I am exercising that choice-making capacity and strengthening it. My vision will become sharper. I will see more clearly, as I go along, what the results of all those choices will be. But understanding is barely half the battle where the making of wise choices is concerned. The will must be engaged too, and for that to happen we must have the second wing: detachment.

There is no more easily misunderstood term in the mystic's lexicon. Detachment is not to be confused with indifference. If you have detachment, you can be affectionate and loving, you can have rich, satisfying relationships, but you will never get caught in *clinging* to people or things in the hope of extracting security.

The fundamental assumption of life today is that nothing is real but the world outside us, reported to us by the senses. And the corollary of that assumption is that you and I are essentially physical beings. But as meditation deepens and you begin to bring the senses under control, you eventually make the startling discovery that you are not your body. Saint Therese of Lisieux, once she had made this discovery, used to describe the body as a kind of envelope, and marvel that so few of us ever try to read the message sealed inside. And her namesake, Teresa of Avila, lamented in a passage I quoted earlier: "We trouble little about carefully preserving the soul's beauty. All our interest is centered in the rough setting of the diamond, the outer wall of the castle – that is to say, in these bodies of ours."

Once you have a measure of detachment from your body, it becomes effortless and natural to act in its best interest – for example, to give it the food it needs and the exercise it requires. You establish a firm but very friendly relationship with the body. Your body will be your "buddy," and it will recognize that you are the boss.

But that's only the beginning. As meditation deepens still further, detachment allows you to realize that you are not your mind either. Up until then, all of us are subject to the whims of body and mind. If our taste buds say, "Fudge brownie *now!*" it is fudge brownie *now*, whatever red warning lights might be flashing in our rearview mirror. And if the mind announces, "I *hate* that person," we have no recourse but to go along for the ride, even though we know it's going to mean a migraine.

With detachment, however, the picture changes. Slowly the physical world loses its hold on you; then, in time, an even more wonderful development comes: the clamorous world of your own emotions loses its hold too. You have come to see that you are not your body; now you realize you are not your mind either. Just as for a short period in meditation you don't hear the cars outside or the planes overhead, there will be periods now when there is no anger in your mind, no clamor of resentment, no matter what may have taken place that day in the office or classroom. It isn't that negative emotions don't arise, but now you can put the storms at a certain distance. In a big thunderstorm, everyone counts the seconds between the lightning bolt and the thunder that follows – one, two, three . . . "Hey, that was close!" Similarly, when you see the lightning inside – a flicker of jealousy or anxiety – and brace yourself for the ensuing turbulence: one, two, three, four, five, six, seven, *eight* . . . And you are surprised to hear only the faintest rumble. "It must be miles and miles away."

Through meditation you can learn to stand back from the heat of mental processes that are raging out of control. When you are too close, when you are too closely identified with the mind, you get badly burned. But as you move back, the heat becomes bearable. The smoke doesn't get in your eyes, so you can see more clearly. Now you find you can *choose* how to respond to a difficult situation.

I'm not unappreciative of the modern psychological methods of dealing with emotional problems like resentment and anxiety, but my own way is different. When I first began to meditate, I was absolutely convinced that I was my mind. But after my meditation deepened, when another person was treating me unkindly and the traditional responses – fight or flight – were right at hand, I could ask myself, "Shall I be rude in return, or shall I treat him kindly? Shall I try to understand his difficulties and support him?" The connection between stimulus and response had been severed, and I saw that I could live in freedom – I could *love* in freedom.

In deep meditation, after many years, you can go to the root of some of the tendencies that have been distorting your life and pluck them out clean. As best I can, I would like to describe how it felt to me the first time this took place.

It was during my summer vacation on the Blue Mountain, treasured months when I had all the time I needed for meditation. I was becoming painfully aware about then of certain weaknesses in myself that had never been apparent to me before I took to meditation. I sat down to meditate one morning and went deep, deep inward. Not a muscle could have been moving. No distraction troubled the mind. "Like the flame of a candle kept in a windless place": that is how the Bhagavad Gita describes the mind of someone who is in deep meditation, and that's exactly how I felt at that moment. There was no movement in the mind – none to the past, none to the future; no images of any kind. All sounds had become inaudible. The senses were closed down. I was experiencing the state Teresa of Avila calls the "prayer of quiet." Consciousness itself was burning steady, motionless, and in its light I could see into the depths of my mind to where a particular weakness was located. I could *see* how long it had been there, how conditioned my mind had become, and how much this weakness had influenced me – not for the best – in my relationships, even in my academic work.

I had reached a deep level where attention, desire, will, and achievement all came together. Having descended to that level, I was able at last to correct that weakness, and in a sense to begin life new thereafter. It was "The End" for old, selfish ways and "Here Beginneth" for new, selfless ones. To paraphrase Meister Eckhart, I went in a pauper – well, not quite, but considerably impoverished – and I came out a prince, wealthy beyond the dreams of avarice.

This dramatic development seemed sudden, but in fact the transformation had been going on for many years. That morning was simply the climax. Saint Bernard of Clairvaux described in his own way this long, baffling, drawn-out process:

> He has quickened my sleeping soul, has aroused and
> softened and goaded my heart, which was in a state of
> torpor and hard as a stone. He has begun to pluck up
> and destroy, to plant and to build, to water the dry
> places, to illuminate the gloomy spots, to throw open
> those which were shut close, to inflame with warmth
> those which were cold, as also to straighten its
> crooked paths and make its rough places smooth. . . .
> In the reformation and renewal of the spirit of my

mind, that is, of my inward man, I have perceived in some degree the loveliness of his beauty.

Meditation renews everything, because it renews the mind itself. Imagine what it would be like this very day to be handed a fresh, new mind – a mind with the dew still on it, one that won't hold resentment or carry hostility. To put it bluntly, resentments are stale food. We don't like to eat day-old bread if we can avoid it, so why should we tolerate week-old feelings and year-old grudges? This renewal of the mind is exactly what takes place each day in deep meditation. You come out of your meditation room in the morning and look around, and never have you seen a buckeye tree as beautiful as the one blooming in your backyard. And listen to that blackbird! You never knew a blackbird could sing so melodiously.

. . . *nothing more courageous* . . .

When we are in the grip of fear, it can feel like a profound paralysis – not at all like the furious agitation that comes with anger or resentment. But experienced meditators deal with fear exactly as they deal with the stormier mental states. They don't analyze; they don't intellectualize. They just leave the neighborhood, traveling deep in meditation to the stillness no wave of fear or anger or greed can disturb. If they find themselves too agitated or too overwhelmed to meditate, they take a fast walk repeating the mantram. The sheer momentum of the effort makes them feel as if they're leaving fear or anger in the dust, and at a deep level – below their conscious awareness – the mantram gradually breaks up the oppressive gridlock of fear or anxiety. Their breathing rhythm alters from shallow and ragged to deep and even. The mind grows steady, and by the time they get home, they are ready to act constructively.

For the illumined man or woman, fear has no meaning. No one is more courageous, and their courage has a very simple origin: once you realize you are not the body, you lose all fear of death. My grandmother was such a person. I was not a very brave boy, but Granny was the bravest person I have ever known, and it was watching her that planted the seeds of my own courage.

I was terribly afraid of death, for example, and in my ancestral home death was not hidden away as it is so often in this country today. When someone in the family died, there was a room right on the first floor of our house called "the dark room" where the body was kept until the cremation could take place. And by tradition, some member of the family had to keep watch there through the night and keep alive the flickering flame of a little oil lamp, so that the body would not be left in darkness.

Nothing could have been more terrifying to me. I couldn't even have considered spending the night in that room, and my cousins gleefully made matters worse by the stories they told of ghosts and demons. But again and again I watched Granny take on this duty without hesitation. She would just lie down on the floor by the side of the dead body, and when I asked her, "Granny, don't you get scared?" she would say, "Why? This is not your Aunt Sita; it is just her body. It's like one of her old saris. There is nothing to be afraid of." And throughout the night she would lie there in the dim light of the coconut oil lamp, repeating her mantram.

This kind of example made a deep, deep impression on me, and after a while my terrible fear of death began to ease. Today I know beyond the shadow of a doubt that I am not my body. My body is a faithful friend, but it is finite – I am not. When I do think about death, I know that when I finally shed my body it will be like a leaf or fruit dropping from the branch: a very natural conclusion to a long, loving, beneficial life.

. . . nothing higher, nothing wider,
nothing more pleasant, nothing fuller
nor better in heaven and earth.

Love is a dynamic process. It is meant to grow. But we have to work at it every day. Even today, after more than forty years of meditation, I work at it still. If there is somebody who gives me offense, I try to be more tender towards that person. When somebody tries to go astray, I try to move closer. It calls for unremitting endeavor.

In the early days of our youth, we all try to seek love through the body. It is a natural beginning, but millions of people get caught on that level and never progress beyond it. I never tell young people, "You haven't any idea what love means." I say, "You are on the first step of love. Let me take you up, step by step. You'll reach the stars, and from there you can love all." The body has its legitimate place, but as an instrument of love it is entirely inadequate. For one thing, to strike a note of grim realism, the body loses its strength with the passage of time; and our need is for a love that will increase without limit.

I've always enjoyed going to weddings. In India, I loved to watch the bride and groom walk together around the sacred fire. In this country, I've been deeply moved by the beautiful exchange of vows and rings. But whenever I hear the words "till death do us part," I feel tempted to stand up and shout to the bride and groom, "No, no, no! Don't accept that!" Love that is physical, death *will* destroy. But love that is spiritual, death can never destroy.

Love can begin as the will of two people to dissolve their separateness over the years until they are not two but one. But even that lofty state is only the beginning of love. It should go on to encompass more and more – friends, relatives, other races, other nations – until finally it embraces all of life. Then you become love itself. And life does not end in death for the person who has become love. That person is not a physical creature, but a beneficial force that can never be extinguished.

Because love is born of God, and cannot rest but in God, above all created things.

It's only when a man or woman of God is well along the spiritual path that they can echo Saint Augustine as Thomas a Kempis does here. You remember Augustine's great outcry, "Thou hast created us for thyself, and our hearts cannot be quieted till they find repose in thee!" Saint Catherine of Genoa speaks the same language: "Because of its capacity for the infinite, the soul could not satisfy itself with earthly things; and the more it strained to do so, the further it moved away from the peace and joy that is God."

There is a growing sense as meditation deepens that this tremendous journey you have undertaken is not to a strange land at all, but to your first and dearest home. As you near journey's end there come moments of recognition, like those of a weary traveler returning home. Something is familiar about that stand of trees up ahead, or the low hills off to your right. The air is fragrant with flowers . . . you can almost remember their names. And your pace quickens: this is where you belong.

Eden, to me, is not a place at all. It is a state of consciousness – that state in which we transcend our physical separateness and become aware of the divine ground of existence within. That is our native state, the place where we really belong. Saint Francis is not Francis of Assisi; he is Francis of Eden. Saint Teresa is not Teresa of Avila; she is Teresa of Eden. They carry Eden around with them. That is why they are at home everywhere, and like superb hosts and hostesses, they want nothing more than for the rest of us to be at home there too.

Theologians have wrangled for nearly two thousand years over the significance of phrases like "the Garden of Eden" and "original sin." No doubt the illumined man or woman could make some astute guesses as to what might have transpired between our spiritual ancestors and a wily serpent; but the more urgent questions, they tell us, concern the here and now. Better to look at the choices we are making right now in our own daily lives and ask whether they are moving us toward Eden or away from it. The Fall is real not because it took place in prehistoric times, but because it happens every single day.

I like to imagine the serpent coming to Adam and Eve to make his pitch. "Listen," he says, "There's nothing like this! All you have to do is look out for number one. You can have your food cooked any way you like. You can have your apartment decorated the way you want it; who cares what anybody else thinks? You can play the kind of music you like as loud as you want, enjoy yourself any way that appeals to you, make piles of money any way you can. Whatever works . . . if it feels good, do it! You don't have to care for *anybody!*" Remarkably similar to the message of our own mass media: happiness lies in complete and utter separateness.

Theologians speak of the Fall, while cosmologists tell us we live in the aftermath of an inconceivably vast explosion called the Big Bang. From a starting point fifteen billion years ago, the effects of the primeval explosion are still detectable by sensitive astronomical instruments: galaxies are still flying apart in all directions. This astronomical model seems a painfully accurate description of life today. Despite all our triumphs in science and technology, I think the human being has never been so distant from other human beings, never so alienated from other living creatures, from the entire environment, and, worst of all, from his or her own self. Propelled by obsessive identification with our own private needs and personalities, we hurtle away from one another at speeds that kill.

Yet in the midst of all this flying apart, this drift toward more and more intense self-will, there is a counterforce: the inward tug of love that is calling us all home.

In Hinduism we have an ancient mythic counterpart to the Fall, and it is very much in harmony with the Big Bang theory too. In the beginning, according to this myth, there was only consciousness: a vast cosmic egg full of unitive awareness. Inexplicably, in a creative burst of differentiation, this cosmic egg exploded in a thousand directions. You and I and all the rest of life are each tiny fragments of that original unity – infinitesimal bits of a vast jigsaw puzzle. Each of us carries with us a tiny bit of the cosmic yolk, a fragment of the divine. And it's that dab of yolk in all of us – the *memory* of unitive consciousness – which keeps us from ever being fully at home in a world of separateness.

Thomas Merton describes this infinitesimal bit of divine yolk in haunting language:

At the center of our being is a point of nothingness which is untouched by sin and by illusion, a point of pure truth, a point or spark which belongs entirely to God, which is never at our disposal, from which God disposes of our lives, which is inaccessible to the fantasies of our mind or the brutalities of our will.

It is this still point which enables us to work tirelessly for the welfare of all, and which draws us inward in the long return to our native state of being.

Chapter Seven

He that loveth, flyeth, runneth and rejoiceth; he is free, and cannot be held in.

He giveth all for all, and hath all in all; because he resteth in One highest above all things, from whom all that is good flows and proceeds.

He respecteth not the gifts, but turneth himself above all goods unto the Giver.

In the early days of meditation, nothing we see in ourselves suggests that we'll ever get off the ground – no wings, no aerodynamic promise of any kind. In the language of Teresa of Avila, we stumble along like poultry, we who were meant to soar like eagles!

But once you have had even a fleeting glimpse of your real home, the tug to return is so powerful that you're like a homing pigeon, with all your attention and all your instincts trained on that shining goal. A stronger will and increased determination will make themselves felt – and you will need them, because as meditation deepens, the obstacles become correspondingly greater. My granny used to say, "The Lord will keep on raising the hurdles – not one inch less than you can jump, but not one inch more either."

In my high school days, there used to be a track meet every year on the eve of summer vacation. Typically, the students who did well in these events were not the exceptional scholars. I was a rather good student, so it was simply assumed that I wouldn't be able to run fast or jump high – or, for that matter, perhaps even walk. But even then, I had a kind of contrary streak: if I found I wasn't good at something, I just had to work at it. So I decided to enter the pole-vaulting event.

I began to practice secretly. Before anyone was up in the morning, I would go and get my pole. I did some experimenting, and soon I discovered there were tricks to pole-vaulting that no one had taught us. On the day of the school games, when the whole village was gathered, everybody looked so pained when I trotted up with my pole! I took my time, gathered my concentration, said my mantram, and took off running. I still remember the gasp of amazement – one doesn't forget these moments! – when I flew like a bird over the bar.

I was able to do this not by reading books about the pole vault, not by admiring other people vaulting, but by trying to do it myself. And that's just how it is with meditation.

He that loveth, flyeth, runneth, and rejoiceth.

Whenever I hear of any great achievement that calls for extraordinary skill and endurance, I'm fascinated by the parallels that emerge with the practice of meditation. A few years ago aviation history was made by two veteran pilots, Dick Rutan and Jeana Yeager, when they flew their specially built airplane the entire distance around the world – a voyage of more than twenty-five thousand miles – without stopping.

Millions of people must have watched the landing on television – not, I think, because it was a spectacle, but because it appeals to our desire for facing challenges and putting ourselves to the test – the same drives that propel us into the practice of meditation. When Rutan was asked why he and his friend had undertaken the trip, he said, "Just for the hell of it." I would say, "Just for the heaven of it," but we mean the same thing. There is no rhyme or reason behind all this, just that deep, driving need to fulfill oneself, to hurl oneself against the greatest imaginable challenge. "When it comes down to it," Rutan added, "this is the ultimate goal: the last plum to be picked."

Friends who were asked to describe Dick Rutan said, "Flying is his life, and his hobby too. He lives and breathes it." That's just what is required for success in meditation. You pool all your resources, fuse them until, like the *Voyager*, you can travel around the whole of life and see it as one unbroken circle. No need to stop; no need to refuel!

You can imagine how much fuel an ordinary aircraft would require to travel around the world. The designer of the *Voyager* – Burt Rutan, Dick's brother – had to make the plane as light as possible to minimize the necessary fuel supply. Just so, in the case of spiritual aspirants, one of the most severe challenges is reducing the weight of self-will to a bare minimum.

When Rutan and Yeager landed, someone asked why they had only fourteen gallons of fuel left. Had they really calculated it that closely? Rutan replied that they had carried considerably more than they would have needed under ideal circumstances. "The problem was we could virtually never fly the plane on its optimum range profile because of weather, winds, and turbulence." The pressure never let up. "Every time we'd take a minute to say 'Hey, this is really neat,' Thor would come out of the sky and run us through a thunderstorm or kill an engine."

This is exactly what happens in the deeper stages of meditation. Even if you have enormous determination and will, you can't be sure it will be enough because you have to provide for storms and turbulence – and for unintended changes of direction and retracing misdirected flight patterns as well. The way to provide this extra measure of fuel is through the conservation of energy; and that is the purpose of sense training. We don't train the senses so we can become ascetics, but simply to give us the fuel we need to make the voyage. To draw the parallel even more closely, it seems that during much of the *Voyager's* flight the fuel gauge was inaccurate. For quite a bit of the trip, they had to fly without even knowing how much fuel they had.

"I've trained all my life for this trip," Dick Rutan said. "It was a major goal of my lifetime. I spent every little bit of experience that I'd gained over a whole life-time of flying to bring this off." If you just replace flying with meditation, you have my story.

The *Voyager,* concluded the *San Francisco Examiner,* "produced a near miracle with a mechanical package of a size that is unimposing. After nine days and 26,000 miles, in history's only nonstop circling of the globe on a single tank of fuel, Dick Rutan and Jeana Yeager eased the slim craft down to a flawless three-point landing. . . . As light as a leaf, the little craft arrived to a luminous backdrop of sun and shadow on the Mojave that fitted the occasion, and Yeager's and Rutan's modesty befitted it also. They came into victory with simple grace."

May we all match their achievement!

He is free, and cannot be held in.

Americans are often surprised to learn that in India, too, boys had the opportunity to be Boy Scouts. We had our official kerchiefs, our khaki shorts, our salute, and our own marching songs. But instead of caps, we wore turbans. And given the kind of wild animals that inhab-ited our forests – lions, tigers, elephants – I would sug-gest that our camping expeditions took considerably more courage than those of the average Scout troop in Cornwall or California.

In order to win a particular merit badge in the Boy Scouts, I had to undergo training in tying knots. I didn't know it at the time, but I could have told my Scoutmaster that all of us are already experts in tying knots. We have hard knots around our hearts – granny knots, reef knots, square knots – and we've tied them ourselves. They are the reason we cannot always be patient, secure, loving, and selfless. The training we need now is in *un*tying knots. When we become aware of the Lord, all the knots become untied. Everything inside becomes loose and free. Then we are able to love everybody, even those who slander us.

Whenever we brood upon ourselves and think only about our own needs, we contract consciousness so tight that it becomes a prison. But if our love and concern are given to others, if we live for the whole instead of just ourselves, no power on earth can inhibit our ability to serve and give.

There is a legend concerning Saint John of the Cross that conveys this priceless truth. John had been imprisoned by persecutors for several months, and as the days and weeks passed and he steadily weakened, he longed more and more to rejoin his spiritual companions, who had placed themselves in his loving care. And finally that selfless desire to rejoin them became so intense that it burst the constraints even of physical laws. Deep in the night, the story goes, he awoke to find his jailer asleep and the doors mysteriously unlocked. Trusting completely in the Lord's guidance, he slipped out of his cell and past more sleeping guards. Somehow he dropped down the sheer rampart and fled towards the river, only to come to a high wall. Trusting still in his guide, he approached the wall and even in his weakened condition climbed it easily. Finally, battered and weary, he arrived at the convent of Teresa and her sisters. In the morning, his jailers were too awestruck even to try to recapture him, for they sensed that he could not have made this escape unaided by God. This has been called miraculous by some; by others, simple proof that when we love very deeply we have access to unlimited strength and wisdom.

Once we've broken out of the prison house of the ego and are able to love everybody whatever they do, we are free. The real meaning of freedom is mastery over our passions and desires. We aren't born with this freedom, but we're all born with the capacity for attaining it. Nothing that anyone did to us in the past, nothing we ourselves have done, can destroy this divine capacity; it is our birthright. Yet, paradoxically, it cannot be fully realized without the cooperation of divine grace. And it takes a long, long time.

He giveth all for all, and hath all
in all . . .

There is a poignant moment in the Gospels when a young man comes running up to Jesus. "Good Master," he says, "how can I win eternal life?" The Lord chastises him tenderly, "Why callest thou me good? There is none good but one, and that is God." Then he answers the young man's question by citing the commandments of Moses. "All these I have observed since my youth!" the fellow blurts out – so full of hope and eagerness.

By now Jesus has noticed that the young man is dressed in fine, expensive clothing. His heart reaches out to him, for he sees his good intentions and sees too what will be his stumbling block. There is a beautiful touch in the narrative: "Jesus, beholding him, loved him." At last he said, "One thing thou lackest; go thy way, sell whatsoever thou hast, and give to the poor, and thou shalt have treasure in heaven: and come, take up the cross and follow me." The young man hears what is being asked, and he cannot give it – at least not then. "He was sad at that saying, and went away grieved: for he had great possessions."

The story can cut us to the quick, for we all have our attachments. Each of us has some counterpart to the wealth that weighed this eager young man down. For some it may be pleasure – midwinter cruises in the Bahamas or a lifetime pass to every concert given by the Grateful Dead. The great mystics see us struggling with attachments like these, and they grow impatient on our behalf. If we could begin to imagine what immense wealth the Lord is trying to pour into our lives, they cry out, we would feel so unutterably foolish, standing here clutching doggedly at our nickel's worth of security. When the Lord offers us our divine inheritance, we reply, "Just put it down over there, and we'll take a look from here." But it is letting go *first* that is the real crux of the spiritual life. No one has said it more boldly than Meister Eckhart:

Know that no man in this life ever gave up so much that he could not find else to let go. Few people, knowing what this means, can stand it long, and yet it is an honest requital, a just exchange. To the extent you eliminate self from your activities, God comes into them, but not more nor less. Begin with that, and let it cost you your uttermost. In this way, and in no other, is true peace to be found.

There is another way of understanding these simple words, "He giveth all for all, and hath all in all." It is this: illumined men and women have complete access to every bit of their vital capacities. They hold all their resources in the hollow of their hands, because they have learned to remain and act completely in the present. They give themselves completely to whatever task they are carrying out, and the astonishing result is that their resources are never depleted.

> *. . . because he resteth in One highest above all things, from whom all that is good flows and proceeds.*

Only the lovers of God are free everywhere and at all times, because their center is in the Lord within. In the practice of meditation we learn how to throw away all other supports. The person who is dependent upon money is not secure: just pull away his pile of bank notes and he will collapse. The person who is dependent on power is not secure: you have only to draw her crutch of power away and she will fall like ninepins. But when we put all those crutches aside and become completely dependent upon God, we are becoming completely dependent upon ourselves. Every day in meditation we renew this magnificent discovery and find, along with Saint Bernard of Clairvaux: "What a great thing is love, provided always that it returns to its origin! Flowing back again into its source it acquires fresh strength to pour itself forth again."

*He respecteth not the gifts, but turneth
himself above all goods unto the Giver.*

Saint Augustine gave a kind of catchall definition of sin that is almost paraphrased in this line of Thomas a Kempis: "All sins are contained in this one category, that one turns away from things divine and truly enduring and turns toward those which are mutable and uncertain."

Last week, as I was passing through Ghirardelli Square in San Francisco, there was a magician performing in the central courtyard. This man had three boxes and a red ball. He opened the boxes, while all of us stood around curious to see what he was going to do. "Come closer," he said, "and watch carefully." And we did. He showed us the box, showed us the ball, then put the ball in the middle box and asked, "May I close the boxes?" "Of course!" we replied. He did so, while we all watched carefully to see if anything went up his sleeve. But nothing did.

Then he asked a young girl to come up and retrieve the red ball. She giggled and confidently opened the middle box. No ball was to be seen! Her jaw dropped and she blushed in surprise. "But I *saw* it go into the box!"

The magician smiled and opened the box on the left – and there, of course, was the ball.

Then he put the ball back into the same box and asked her to open it. Again there was the initial confidence, again the look of complete astonishment. Again and again he did the trick – she still hadn't learned.

I couldn't help thinking that this is one of the cruel tricks life plays on every one of us. "I was sure happiness was there. I could almost touch it!" Over the last thirty years, so many young friends have assured me they have found the way to happiness and have gone off to pursue it. After a time they have come back brokenhearted – and then gone back and done the same thing a little later. They look just like this young girl – astonished, bewildered, full of consternation.

Being myself something of an amateur magician, I know some of the trade secrets. One is that if I can get you to watch my right hand closely, I can do what I like with the left. In the deeper stages of meditation, when Life the Magician says, "Hey, Greg, here's the red ball going into this box. Wouldn't you like to open it?" Greg can just sit back and say, "Nope."

"Why not?"

"Because I know the ball's not there."

Greg has left sorrow behind.

What the great mystics are trying to convey is the enormous contrast between the evanescent pleasures of the physical world, which can never, ever satisfy us, and the unbounded joy of loving God.

Again, no one has expressed this more powerfully than Saint Augustine: "What do I love when I love my God? Not the beauty of any bodily thing, nor the fair harmony of time, nor the brightness of the light, . . . nor sweet melodies of varied songs, nor limbs acceptable to embracements of flesh. None of these I love when I love my God; and yet I love a kind of light, and melody, and fragrance, and embracement, when I love my God."

With beautiful words and ardent passion, Augustine is saying that the love of God satisfies our hunger always. When Jesus said to the woman at the well, "I am thirsty," she gave him water. But instead of thanking her, he spoke to her as only a great spiritual teacher can: "Whosoever drinketh of this water shall thirst again, but whosoever drinketh of the water that I shall give him shall never thirst." All physical pleasures come to an end swiftly, but the joy that comes from the love of God only increases with time.

Chapter Eight

Love oftentimes knoweth no measure,
but is fervent beyond all measure.

Love feels no burden, thinks nothing
of trouble, attempts what is above
its strength, pleads no excuse of
impossibility; for it thinks all things
lawful for itself and all things possible.

It is therefore able to undertake all
things; and it completes many things,
and warrants them to take effect, where
he who does not love would faint and
lie down.

When we can withdraw our attention from problems, they become light; but selfishness makes everything a terrible burden. Even something that is very light will become terrible, nearly impossible, when our reserves of love and compassion are running low. It is only when we give the Lord within all our love and devotion that we can say with Thomas, "Love is able to undertake all things."

I was reminded the other day of what the love of the

Lord within can do for us. We were at the beach when my wife, Christine, spotted a little seal slowly looking around to see whether it had an audience. When it saw two enthusiastic spectators it performed a few numbers, including a figure eight. It came even closer and raised its bald head above the water, looking right at us with those bright eyes as if asking us to join it. Then again it began frolicking just for the sake of frolicking, diving for the pure love of diving.

At the same time I noticed two starfish lying flat on the shore, and I felt awfully sorry for them. I could imagine one saying, "How I wish I could jump and play and dive in the sea like that baby seal!" and the other replying, "You took the words right out of my mouth." While I watched, a wave came and washed them back into the sea they must have been longing for.

When we look at the life of Jesus, Thomas would say, it should bring out this longing in our hearts to be a little like Jesus. In some mysterious way, when this longing becomes deeper and deeper, all desires are withdrawn from the evanescent foam and froth of life to feed this huge desire. We lie there supine on the sand, longing and longing, and at last a great wave of grace comes and picks us up like those starfish. In other words, we need to put sustained effort into the spiritual life, but what really enables us to become aware of the Lord at last is only his infinite mercy.

Love oftentimes knoweth no measure, but is fervent beyond all measure.

Love has nothing to do with ledger sheets or bottom-line accounting. Love doesn't keep records, and refuses to hire a bookkeeper. Real love has no limits, because it springs from boundless depths.

Whenever you are tempted to calculate, "If I give sixty grams of love, how much will I get in return?" love becomes a contract. For love to be a sacrament, we should be able to stand firm and steadfast each day and say, "Whether you like me or hate me, whether you light up when I enter the room or leave it at the first opportunity, I am going to love you more and more." Love doesn't insist upon reciprocity, and it never counts the cost.

Love feels no burden, thinks nothing of trouble, attempts what is above its strength, pleads no excuse of impossibility . . .

I was always capable of hard, sustained work, and in the early years of my own spiritual practice I drew heavily on that capacity. I changed all my ways, reversing long-standing patterns of living, and I took great joy in doing so. As I worked my way down to the more stubborn attachments, I found it harder going, but I kept at it anyway. Finally, however, I reached a point when I felt I could go no further. What I was attempting to do appeared now to be quite literally impossible. The rest of the journey seemed completely beyond me – beyond any human being. I was plunged into grief.

Since then I have come to understand that every man or woman who has sought God-realization has undergone this anguish, that it comes at a certain stage in the spiritual journey.

For a long time, you see, you are just struggling across the foothills of the spiritual Himalayas, longing for at least a glimpse of one of those snowy peaks. A mantle of early morning frost on a good-sized hill sets your heart racing, and that night you can hardly bear to stop and camp. You forge on, and at last before you beckons a snowcapped peak – the real thing this time – and everything in you is bent on scaling it. You want with all your heart to get there, but right in front of you yawns a chasm that is miles across. "What do I do now?" you ask. "There is no road! There isn't even a track for a mountain goat. Even if I have tremendous willpower and energy, how can I travel if there is no path?" You see the peak and the chasm at just the same moment. Intense restlessness seizes you, and wild optimism alternating with despair.

People who depend on their own sheer willpower can get into trouble at this stage. But if from the earliest days of your spiritual life you have tried, like Brother Lawrence, to keep yourself in the presence of God through meditation and repetition of the Holy Name, you know what to do. With the trust and affection of a small child, you turn to the Lord of Love within and ask, "Why don't you just take me up in your arms and deposit me on the other side? I'll close my eyes and repeat your name, and leave the rest to you!"

And this is what takes place. It happened to me, and it can happen to you. Love wells up in your heart if you surrender your self-will, and devotion carries you across the chasm. You don't even feel the motion. You think you're still on the frostbitten lower slopes; then after a while you open your eyes and find yourself on the snowcapped peak. Finally it dawns on you, "I don't have to do any leaping. Whenever there is a great leap to be made, the Lord is there to take me in his arms, cradle me against his chest, and deposit me safely."

Years later, looking back on all this, I have realized that I am a very blessed creature. I am still lost in wonder at what happened to me, for I know that I could never have completed the journey under my own power. It was grace alone that enabled me to continue until the end.

This mystery has been recorded again and again in the lives of the mystics. Teresa of Avila writes in her commentary on the Song of Songs:

An infant doesn't understand how it grows, nor does it know how it gets its milk; for without its sucking or doing anything, often the milk is put into its mouth. Likewise, here, the soul is completely ignorant. It knows neither how nor from where that great blessing came to it, nor can it understand . . . it sees that it is nourished and made better and doesn't know when it deserved this. It is instructed in great truths without seeing the Master who teaches it; fortified in virtues and favored by One who knows it well. . . . It doesn't know what to compare his grace to, unless to the great love a mother has for her child in nourishing and caressing it.

In playful language we can never forget, Sri Ramakrishna, the great Bengali saint of the nineteenth century, speaks of the same experience. He says that in the first half of our spiritual endeavors, we are like baby monkeys. The little monkey holds on to its mother while she jumps from branch to branch, and he has to hold tight because if he loosens his grip, down he'll fall. But during the second half, Ramakrishna says, we are like kittens. The mother cat doesn't expect her kitten to hold on to her; she picks him up by the scruff of the neck. You would think she is being cruel to hold him like that; but in fact she is being very protective. The kitten just goes limp and lets the mother cat do the traveling. And when the kitten is set down on his feet again, the mother's protective love continues to surround him. He can be right on the verge of making what the feline world sees as a serious mistake, but the mother won't let him. Have you seen a mother cat reach out and slap the kitten with her paw? It *hurts*, and the kitten doesn't make that mistake again!

This is how faith takes root in our heart and grows. Sometimes people speak of faith as something we should cultivate on principle – no matter how the intellect balks, no matter what our own experience has taught us. My own attitude is stubbornly practical. I've never taken anything on faith that I could not test against my own experience. Today, I would say freely that I am a man of profound faith in God. But mine is a *living* faith. It began as the most tentative proposition: "I shall move in this direction, even when it doesn't look pleasant, and let us see what happens." As my meditation deepened, great difficulties did come my way, but over and over I have been rescued – sometimes at the eleventh hour. I could never have told you why, but my path would be cleared; courage, insight, and resourcefulness would come to me. Today, after many years of validation in my personal experience, I can claim that my faith in God has become unshakable. But that faith is the fruit of a long period of effort and clear observation – and, I would add, an open mind.

The poet Robert Browning uses a geometrical simile: all the Lord expects us to do is to draw the arc; the Lord himself will complete the circle. Have I done everything possible to train my senses, to subdue my passions, to liquidate my self-will? If I have, even if I have not been completely successful, he will augment my strivings and reward my efforts a hundredfold.

. . . for it thinks all things lawful for itself and all things possible.

G. K. Chesterton was a Catholic writer who wrote the delightful Father Brown mysteries and a beautiful book on Saint Francis of Assisi. It may have been Saint Francis's life that inspired Chesterton to write:

Loving means to love that which is unlovable,
        Or it is no virtue at all.
Forgiving means to pardon the unpardonable,
Faith means believing the unbelievable,
And hoping means to hope when things are hopeless.

This is what the practice of meditation enables you to do.

It is therefore able to undertake all things; and it completes many things, and warrants them to take effect, where he who does not love would faint and lie down.

When you have learned to travel far, far inside through meditation, and to place yourself at the feet of the Lord, you are able to tap into enormous reservoirs of love and wisdom. You have an ally now with *deep* pockets. Once you have succeeded in aligning your own will with the will of the Lord, you have made yourself invincible.

It is not that we are extraordinary people. But within us there are tremendous forces of which we are all but ignorant – forces as mighty as cosmic radiation or electromagnetism or the solar wind. We could ally ourselves with these internal forces, but we don't really believe they are there. Saint Francis de Sales, a French mystic of the seventeenth century, wrote, "Our free will can hinder the course of inspiration, and when the favorable gale of God's grace swells the sails of our soul, it is in our power to refuse consent."

In other words, propelling our boat across the sea is not our responsibility; the wind will do that. But we do have to set the sails and keep our boat yare, as sailors say. I am certain that Francis de Sales would also tell us it isn't enough just to set the sail and then go below and read *Lord Jim* for the rest of the voyage. At every stage in meditation, we need to be dedicating ourselves anew to all the disciplines. It's very much like the constant work aboard a ship at sea. The boat might be sailing along without any visible effort on anyone's part, but on deck and below there's likely to be a lot of activity. One sailor is mending sails, another is putting tar over all the cracks, still others are swabbing the decks or oiling the fittings or making sure the lines are secured. On long voyages there are periods of deadly, boring, uneventful work. For long stretches of time in meditation, too, you can't really see any progress. But when a great tropical storm bears down upon your little ship – storms of anger, fear, or greed – and not so much as a keg of molasses gets washed overboard, you feel rewarded. All that dull, dreary labor has paid off.

To re-ignite enthusiasm when it is slowly fading, the best thing you can do is to spend time with a passionately enthusiastic teacher. If you can visit him or her in person, that is ideal, but even to spend an hour reading someone like Teresa of Avila can lift you out of your doldrums. It's as if she were to stride right into your little room, look around, and say, "It's too dark in here. Let me give you a two-hundred-watt bulb!"

A spiritual teacher can help you by a kind of osmosis. But they can help you very practically, too, by giving you a thousand and one tips for tightening up the ship. It's all little, little things, but the sum total is what determines the quality of your meditation. You may have gone over the instructions in meditation over and over again and feel there is nothing more to learn, but you still need to review them regularly. The deeper significance of some of those instructions will not be clear until you have been practicing meditation over a long period of time. That is why, although I have already touched upon most of the eight disciplines I recommend for meditation, I'd like to go into some of the finer points now.

First, have your morning meditation as early as possible, and be as regular about it as you can. Most of us get hungry for breakfast at a particular time; soon you will find you get hungry for meditation at a particular time, too. As John of Kronstadt said, "Prayer is the breathing of the soul. Prayer is our spiritual food and drink." At the time when you would normally be settling down and starting a passage, the mind begins to draw inward of its own volition, no matter where you are. You'll feel a restlessness, a strong pull toward the room or corner you have set aside for meditation – and this is just how it should be.

Second, there is the recurring problem of sleep in meditation. As soon as your neuromuscular system begins to relax, there is a tendency to let go. Don't yield to those waves of drowsiness, no matter how delicious they seem. Be sure there is fresh air coming into the room and that you haven't gotten too comfortable. If you still feel you need tea or coffee, determine just how much will help keep you alert and don't drink more than that. Jumps and jitters aren't a great improvement over sleepiness.

Even when you've taken all these precautions, you may feel the passage drifting away like a kite whose string is slipping through sleepy fingers. Dimly, you see the kite zigzagging across the sky, and then it's lost. As soon as you feel this happening, move away from the back support and sit up straighter. If necessary, open your eyes for a moment and repeat the Holy Name, but do not yield to sleep. If you do, some of the later transitions in meditation will be much more difficult.

Third, keep memorizing new inspirational passages. Don't be content with just a few. Any passage can get stale with long use, but you can keep your favorites fresh for years so long as you have a repertoire of new ones on hand. This is very much like going over your ropes, like a sailor or a climber, and being sure none of them is frayed.

It's one thing to know you need new passages and it's another to carve out time in a busy life to memorize them. You may wait in vain for enough free hours to commit the entire "Wonderful Effects of Divine Love" to memory. But five minutes will open up here and there. Just keep handy an index card on which you've copied part or all of the passage you're currently working on. Don't be discouraged if at first you find it hard to memorize passages. Memory is like a muscle. You can build it up.

Fourth, there is the problem of distractions. They will be a challenge in meditation from the earliest weeks until the most advanced stages, and in warning you about yielding to them, I'll be as firm as Theophan the Recluse: "You must not allow your thoughts to wander at random, but as soon as they run away you must immediately bring them back."

Let us be absolutely clear: any thought, any idea, any association or image, *anything* that comes into your mind beyond the words of the passage itself is a distraction and has to be treated as a distraction. The anonymous author of the fourteenth-century mystical treatise *The Cloud of Unknowing* tells us exactly why: distractions can come with rosaries in their hands!

> It is inevitable that ideas will arise in your mind and try to distract you in a thousand ways. . . . Dispel them by turning to Jesus with loving desire. Don't be surprised if your thoughts seem holy. . . . But if you pay attention to any of these ideas, they will have gained what they wanted of you. . . . Soon you will be thinking about your sinful life, and perhaps in this connection you will recall some place where you have lived in the past, until suddenly before you know it your mind is completely scattered.

Distractions come in a thousand attractive shapes and colors. One of the chief sources is the innate human tendency to fantasize. It isn't only abnormal people who fantasize; everybody does. All these millions of people buying lottery tickets are thinking, "When I win the jackpot, the first thing I'll buy is . . ."

The mystics describe this impulse to fantasize as almost a zone in consciousness, a region you travel through as you move deeper in meditation. "As we pass from without to within," says Theophan the Recluse, "we first encounter the powers of imagination and fantasy." These powers are heightened in meditation, and they can paint very alluring pictures. Especially if you're artistic, it is tempting just to stay in fantasy land, build a little cottage, and never take a step further.

Anyone who has tried to meditate even a little can attest to the fantasizing power of the mind, and anyone who knows anything of *life* knows what havoc that power can wreak. We have a simple but profound story in India about a milkmaid who is going to the village with a pot of milk on her head. While walking she thinks, "I like dancing, and when I sell my milk I'm going to buy dancing bells. I'll fasten them to my ankles so they make music whenever I move, and when I dance —!" She starts to dance, the pot falls, and the milk she was going to sell is gone. The story applies to every one of us, for we all have our own equivalent of dancing bells and pots of milk.

Once you decide to take the problem of distractions in hand, you make some interesting discoveries. First, you find that often distractions will enter through association. A particular phrase or word in the passage might be highly charged for you, so that it is like a door that suddenly swings open and lets the mind run out. There are few thrills quite as satisfying as waiting quietly with concentration, going through the passage, and catching the mind just as it starts to steal away. Now you know to put up a sign there: "Wrong Way, No Exit."

You also gradually discover that just before a distraction comes, your concentration will begin to flicker a little. That very flicker can usher in a wave of restlessness, anger, or fear. It requires great capacity and years of experience to observe this: the mind is almost on the passage but not quite settled, and just coming up is that split second when concentration might be lost. Unless the party of distractions (they don't usually come alone; they travel with lots of relatives) see this kind of opening, they won't try to come in. Once you have observed all this for yourself, you'll have all the motivation you need to sit up straighter and give more concentration. That's all you have to do. Don't try to fight the distractions off. Just strengthen the defense.

Even with the best of efforts, even for experienced meditators, the passage will sometimes slip away. Without knowing how you got there, you find yourself back downtown, walking along your favorite boulevard while your eyes dart pleasurably into the shop windows. When this happens, don't gnash your teeth or get depressed. Just bring the mind back – quietly, firmly – to the beginning of the passage. This is a simple but highly effective discipline. The first few times I invoked it, my mind would cry out, "No! Oh, no, not that!" It might even have had the nerve to add, "It's not fair." But once my mind saw I was unmoved, the mid-meditation excursions were over.

The purpose of all these tactics, of course, is to enable you to go through the words of the inspirational passage with complete concentration. Saint John of the Ladder states it clearly: "You must make a great effort to confine your mind within the words of the prayer." It will take years, but once you have perfected this skill no distraction will be able to enter your mind. It can come and knock on the door; you will not open it. It can ring the bell; you will just turn the volume of the passage up louder. This is what Saint Teresa did; this is what Saint Francis did. They just kept turning up the volume until it became so loud in the depths of consciousness that all distractions were drowned.

Today, when I use the words "Lord, make me an instrument of thy peace," they resonate at a deep, deep level. It is no longer a matter of words; it is now a great desire encased in words – and desire is power. When the Prayer of Saint Francis discharges its power at a deep level, you will slowly start behaving like Francis. Instead of wanting other people to console you, you will start consoling them. Instead of nursing old grievances, you will be more forgiving. You will stand up and face opposition calmly, neither flinching nor retaliating. You will become a Little Flower of South Bend, or of Minneapolis!

"It is in giving that we receive," says Saint Francis, and when these words have come to life in your heart, you keep on giving with one hand while the Lord is putting it in your other hand. You don't have to look back and ask, "Is it exhausted? Am I on the last round?"

This experience of infinite spiritual wealth is what Thomas a Kempis means when he says love is "able to undertake all things." When this great wealth pours into our hands, we cannot hold onto it for our own ends. If we've been given greater energy, we're expected by the Lord to use it to help and support others. If we didn't return these gifts in selfless work, we would be tormented by restlessness. Because we have limitless love pouring out from our hearts, endless energy driving our lives, we need to give it to everyone who comes in contact with us.

So don't look to any kind of sensation, bodily or emotional, as a sign that your meditation is deepening. The real test is, "How much am I able to love? How much am I able to give, even at my own expense, even when it is painful?" In her great work on prayer, *The Way of Perfection*, Teresa of Avila says, "Progress has nothing to do with enjoying the greatest number of consolations in prayer, or with raptures, visions, or favors. . . ." We want to ask, "Then what *does* spiritual progress mean?" And later Teresa gives us her answer: "For my own part, I believe that love is the measure of our ability to bear crosses."

Chapter Nine

Love is watchful, and sleeping slumbereth not.

Though weary, it is not tired; though pressed, it is not straitened; though alarmed, it is not confounded; but as a lively flame and burning torch, it forces its way upwards, and securely passes through all.

If any man love, he knoweth what is the cry of this voice. For it is a loud cry in the ears of God, the mere ardent affection of the soul, when it saith, "My God, my love, thou art all mine, and I am all thine."

When we love the Lord, when we want to serve him and realize him, most of the things we call deprivations will become enrichments. Most of what we now call denials will become affirmations.

In the deepest stages of meditation, there comes the moment when it is not enough to love Christ the teacher and friend: we want to unite ourselves with Christ in his suffering, to relieve him of it, to share it. The way we do this is to relieve the suffering of those around us. The Buddha told his disciples, "Just as a mother with her own life protects her child – her *only* child – from harm, so let your love flow outward to the universe – a limitless love, without hatred or enmity."

Love is watchful, and sleeping slumbereth not.

Increasingly as we grow older, sleep can become problematic. Old memories come to stalk us; fears and resentments come to nibble at our security. Sleep may be a long time coming, and when it comes it is often shattered by unpleasant dreams. Small wonder that people spend five hundred million dollars each year on sleeping pills. Small wonder they come to dread going to bed at night.

But the great mystics speak very differently of both sleep and sleeplessness.

The German mystic Angelus Silesius wrote in beautiful, enigmatic language that almost echoes Thomas: "The light of splendor shines in the middle of the night. Who can see it? A heart which has eyes and watches."

Of course, the light he is describing is not physical, and the night is not only the stretch of time between sunset and sunrise. What you are doing in meditation is trying to make the unconscious conscious: to travel deep into the dark realms of the unconscious and set them ablaze with spiritual awareness. You do this in a small way each time you meditate, but you also enter the unconscious when you go to sleep at night, and one of the remarkable discoveries you will make as your meditation deepens is that you can make considerable progress during your sleep. Later on, in fact, some of the most thrilling experiences to come your way are likely to take place not during meditation and not during the day, but in the middle of the night.

This is why I place so much emphasis on a simple bedtime sequence that everyone can follow with benefit, whether their desire is for spiritual awareness or just the blessed gift of a sound night's sleep. First, put away your Agatha Christie or John le Carré. The last things you read about, or think about, or see on television, will follow you into your sleep and color your dreams.

Second, spend fifteen minutes to half an hour reading something of genuine inspirational value – ideally, works from the great mystical traditions. (Dame Agatha Christie would very likely agree with this advice: a friend told me recently that Miss Marple herself always read a few lines from Thomas a Kempis before bedtime.) When you have finished, turn off your light and begin repeating your mantram, giving it all the attention you can, and keep repeating it until you fall asleep.

To do this is much harder than it sounds. It is terribly difficult, in fact, because the period just before sleep is like listening in on a party line. Someone is talking on one line about the happenings of the day, while on another a voice keeps harping on your mistakes and shortcomings, and still a third is chattering away about tomorrow. To keep your attention on the Holy Name when all this is going on is hard, hard work. For many nights, you may not be falling asleep in your mantram at all; you'll be drifting off into your own thoughts.

If this happens, don't get discouraged; be patient and keep on trying. For just at the juncture of waking and sleeping there is a narrow entry into the unconscious, and if at that instant you are repeating the Holy Name, it will slip inside. When you have learned to fall asleep in the mantram, you may sometimes hear it in your sleep. When a nightmare is slowly tiptoeing in, the mantram will reverberate and the nightmare will vanish. All night long the name of the Lord can go on echoing, "Jesus, Jesus, Jesus," and as it does, old wounds are healed and long-standing conflicts are resolved. Diffidence gives way to confidence, and despair to faith.

In India we have a holiday called *Shivaratri,* "the night of Lord Shiva." On this night everybody, including the children, tells the Lord, "Every night you have to stay awake to keep an eye on us. But tonight we promise to be good so that you can sleep." We go to the temple and we spend the whole night there, repeating our mantram, singing songs of devotion, and listening to spiritual discourses so that the Lord can sleep without worrying about what we're up to.

Of course, the deeper meaning that is supposed to dawn upon us one day is, "Hey, instead of just one night, why don't we make it one week?" Then, when you have been good for one week – being selfless, putting everybody first – the Lord says "I'm beginning to feel so rested, I haven't felt this good in years. Shall we do it for one month now?" You groan, "How did I get into this?" But your spiritual life has really begun now. Finally, when you can say, "Even in my sleep I cannot feel a wave of anger or resentment against anybody," you have reached the level of spiritual awareness where every night is Shivaratri.

There is a similar episode in the life of young Therese of Lisieux. She was so devoted to Jesus, so close to him, that she thought of him as a child who was her joyful companion. This sweet devotion concealed an underlying strength, for even in times of adversity her love did not waver. Speaking about a painful period of aridity, she says, "Jesus was sleeping as usual in my little boat; ah, I see very well how rarely souls allow him to sleep peacefully within them. Jesus is so fatigued with always having to take the initiative and to attend to others that he hastens to take advantage of the repose I offer to him."

Though weary, it is not tired; though pressed, it is not straitened; though alarmed, it is not confounded . . .

Here Thomas is making a mature and realistic assessment of the latter stages of the spiritual life. He warns that it's far from a bed of roses. It's not a vacation from life with all expenses paid. There will be exhaustion, he promises, anxiety, and frustration – all the mental states you might have thought you'd left behind. Only now you have some control over the mind, as well as a tremendous purpose toward which you are working. You know that these negative states will pass, that none of them can overwhelm you, because you know they exist only in the mind. This is why the famous "bookmark prayer" of Saint Teresa of Avila offers such tender consolation, and why it is such a useful passage for meditation:

> Let nothing upset you;
> Let nothing frighten you.
> Everything is changing;
> God alone is changeless.
> Patience attains the goal.
> Who has God lacks nothing;
> God alone fills all our needs.

"Though weary," says Thomas, love "is never tired." You see, as soon as you get some control over your thinking process, energy is released. Thinking consumes a *lot* of energy, but you never really discover this until the titanic factory of the mind closes down. When it does close down, and all the tremendous racket of the thinking process is hushed, the body benefits immediately. Vitality that isn't tied up in thinking goes to the body directly. The mind will say, "I don't need it now. You take it as a loan, but be sure you use it wisely." That is why, when you are meditating deeply and well, you can throw yourself tirelessly into selfless work. You may get weary, but the fuel tank is never drained.

Most of the time, I believe, what tires us out is not the

work we do or the challenging conditions under which we do it. What really exhausts us is wanting to get something from it for ourselves. When we are entirely free from selfish desires, there is no longer a difference between rest and activity. Mahatma Gandhi described this remarkable state as follows: "Our very sleep is action, for we sleep with the thought of God in our hearts. . . . This restlessness inspired by God constitutes true rest."

Though pressed, it is not straitened . . .

Worry is probably the most energy-*in*efficient activity the mind is prone to. By deepening meditation, you can curtail its excessive claims on your time and vitality. You might sit down for meditation feeling burdened by terrible problems, but as you give your attention more and more to the Prayer of Saint Francis, the burden mysteriously lifts, and at the end of your meditation you find you have left all your anxieties at the feet of the Lord. The problem might still be there, but now you have the resources to begin to solve it wisely and selflessly. Gradually, when you have experienced this again and again, there comes the lively awareness that you are equal to any problem that may come to you, because you know the Lord is within, waiting to help.

Though alarmed, it is not confounded . . .

In the parts of India that are watered by the great monsoons, there are essentially two seasons – the wet season and the hot season. During the hot season, the whole earth is parched for six months, from December to June. The heat is scorching. Everywhere you see trees thirsting for water, animals panting for something to drink. By the end of May people are scanning the horizon, and when they meet at the temple or market they ask, "Did you see the monsoon cloud yesterday?" At first it's no larger than a fist, but slowly it becomes bigger and bigger, until finally it fills the whole sky, dark almost as the night. When at last the monsoon bursts, the whole sky lights up and there is a tremendous thunderclap. There is joy in this thunder, which is the rain saying, "I am coming! I am coming!"

Indian mystics who come from the monsoon regions love to allude to these great storms to describe their own experiences in meditation – especially to the long wait *before* the storms. As meditation deepens, there are periods universally called "dry spells." The feeling of deprivation can be so terrible that you feel you are trudging through a real Sahara. Whatever you get, whatever comes to you, only intensifies your longing. "My soul thirsteth for thee," King David lamented. "My flesh also longeth after thee, in a barren and dry land where no water is."

These periods are painful, but they are absolutely necessary. A spiritual experience cannot take place until there has been a certain strengthening of desire. Our love has to be intense, irresistible, sustained all the time. It isn't just a question of time and regular effort, but of *passion*.

Most people, I've observed, have a great many desires. And, because they are many, each desire in itself is rather small. These many desires are accordingly rather easy to satisfy – at least on a short-term basis. The effect of the mass media is to turn almost all of us into people with many desires. The principle behind it is simple: the more things we can be made to want, the more things we will buy. Ideally, we can be persuaded to invest in scuba diving equipment in July, a motorboat in August, and an indoor gym in September. It is the job of the mass media to multiply and proliferate our desires.

Yet I have also observed that in spite of the best efforts of Madison Avenue, there are a number of men and women who have only *some* desires. Because these desires are fewer, each one is bigger. These people with only some desires want satisfactions that last. They can't be manipulated as easily as those whose desires are many. They'll set their own goals.

But there is an even smaller group of people, rather rare: those who have just a *few* desires. My attention is always drawn to these people. If they are students, I can usually predict they will be at the top of their class. From their ranks come great scientists and brilliant artists – real benefactors of the human race.

Finally, there is that rarest type of all, the person who has only *one* unbounded desire which nothing on the face of the earth can satisfy. All his vitality has come into his hands; all her attention is focused like a laser. When I meet someone like this, I can predict with accuracy,

"That person will not be content with anything less than realizing God. He or she will accept no substitute." From this smallest band of all, down through time, have come men and women like Teresa of Avila, Francis of Assisi, and Mahatma Gandhi.

You should not grieve if you can't honestly put yourself in this last category. Right this minute you may be riddled with many, many small desires; but gradually, through the sincere, sustained practice of difficult spiritual disciplines, you can reduce many desires into some, then some into a few, and ultimately a few into one all-consuming passion. At that point nothing finite will satisfy you: not being the head of a great country, not amassing billions of dollars, not landing in the Andromeda galaxy – nothing.

For the vast majority of ordinary people like us, it takes a long, long time to unify desires. We must be prepared for many years, even decades, of taking the energy from old desires and pouring it into this new stream. It is painful. But that's the way it is in all training, whether it is for tennis or ballet or self-realization. Don't you say, "No pain, no gain"? It is the capacity to hold out to the very end that enables us to grow to our full stature.

As we near the goal, as our desires are becoming more and more unified, the very strength of our yearning begins to draw the Lord toward us. The Lord just cannot resist the longing of someone who is deeply devoted, and from time to time, he reveals himself in the depths of that person's consciousness. In the words of John Tauler, "When we thus clear the ground and make our soul ready, without doubt God must fill up the void."

When the monsoon cloud of grace bursts, there is no thrill like it in the world. In a second you forget all the torment of waiting, and you say, "I am never going to let you go. I am going to keep my arms around you all the time." Yet the first visits of the Beloved are fleeting. An instant and he is gone – a brief, thirst-quenching shower, and then the long drought again. It is a stunning disappointment which has fallen upon every mystic. Desolate, you throw yourself down with your heart broken into a thousand pieces, and once again there is the watching, the waiting, and the painful drawing in of all your desires.

So when grace comes, don't get excited and tell all the world, "I'm in a state of grace." You won't be for long!

There is no avoiding these long stretches of aridity, because they are part of spiritual growth. But you can safeguard yourself against feeling overwhelmed or defeated when they come your way. The key is to train the mind from the earliest days not to get elated by victories or depressed by setbacks. The mind is always on the lookout for a chance to get excited. "Did you see that, boss? I managed to stay right there on the passage for fifteen minutes straight. Let's celebrate!" An hour later, it is just as ready to wallow in despair. "I'll never be able to walk past a bakery unscathed, *never!* Let's find a bridge and jump off." Your job is to nip both kinds of reaction in the bud.

Finally, years later, when we are united with the Lord permanently, we ask, "How could you, who are called the Lord of Love, have been so cruel? How could you have toyed with me so?"

And the Lord will smile his beautiful, enigmatic smile and ask, "How else could I have unified your desires?"

But as a lively flame and burning torch, it forces its way upwards, and securely passes through all.

When I was a boy, there were dense forests near my native village in South India. In these forests wild animals roamed at will, and out of fear of these creatures most people didn't go out at night if they could avoid it. When they did have to go out, they would carry large torches made of coconut fiber soaked in oil. These torches burned slowly, and cast so bright a glow that you could see the path quite easily. There was no fear of stepping on a cobra, and the larger animals ran the other way as soon as they saw the approaching flame.

Men and women of God are like these torches. They shed brightness wherever they go, dispelling all fears. In the Hindu and Buddhist tradition, our real Self is described as *deva,* from a Sanskrit root meaning "light" with which the English word *divine* is related. Our real Self is regarded as the source of all light. The deeper we go in meditation, the nearer we get to this light and the brighter its glow appears. Jacapone da Todi, a Franciscan mystic of the thirteenth century, describes it in ecstatic poetry: *Lume fuor di mesura / Resplende nel mio core*, "Light without measure shines in my heart."

Once you've caught even a glimpse of this light, you will want each day to see more of it and to bring more of it into your life. Finally you won't just see the light; you will become the light yourself. Saint Teresa of Avila, who is to me the most glamorous woman the West has produced, carried the light of spiritual awareness all over Spain, undaunted by serious ailments any one of which would send most of us to the infirmary. She said of herself that she lived in the light that knows no night.

Although many Western mystics have dropped glorious hints as to how this state can be reached, none have spelled it out more clearly than the saints of the Eastern Orthodox tradition. In nineteenth-century Russia, Theophan the Recluse wrote:

> The more [the aspirant] strives to pray, the more thoughts will quieten down, and the purer prayer will become. . . . But the atmosphere of the soul is not purified until a small spiritual flame is kindled in the soul. This flame is the work of the grace of God. This flame appears when a man or woman has attained a certain measure of purity in the general moral order of his life. Yet it is not permanent, but blazes up and then down and its burning is not of an even strength. But no matter how dimly or brightly it burns, this flame of love is always there, always ascends to the Lord and sings a song to him.

To light this flame and keep it lit, the mystics draw upon an endless source of fuel – the power that is contained in sexual desire, which is the equivalent in the human being of a tremendous oil well. It might seem perplexing to think of desire as fuel, but think of what great lengths we will go to in order to satisfy our desires. That is why I never speak negatively about sex. To me, sex is a storehouse of power. It is our wealth. Strong sexual urges are natural, but they can be trained – and they must be.

The sex drive is the "crude oil" of consciousness. Refined, it can take us all the way to the goal of life. It is so raw and powerful that it seems unfair that we should have to master it. But only a power of this magnitude will carry us to the summit of consciousness. It is said in our Hindu scriptures that when the sex faculty comes under complete control, all the vitality that has been consolidated travels through the physical system nourishing the vital organs, strengthening the immune system, and prolonging creativity into the very twilight of life.

There are a few rare individuals who seem to achieve mastery over their sexual desires with no apparent struggle, but for the vast majority it takes many years. It is a gradual development, and sex has a special significance at each stage in life. As we pass from childhood to the teen years, then to our twenties and thirties, to middle age and old age, there is a gradual evolution of the way we should look at sex and the way we should use it. It grieves me to notice how many older people retain their teenage attitudes toward sex. It keeps surprising me, because by the time we are forty all our *other* attitudes have changed. We don't play the games children play; we don't undertake the exploits teenagers do. We seem to have grown in most aspects, but not in our understanding of sex.

The media have a great deal to do with this immaturity where sex is concerned. If you have grown up in this country, you may simply accept the continuous propaganda that is going on. Movies and television programs, as well as advertisements for all kinds of products, inundate us with sexually charged messages and images. All of this conditioning is particularly tragic when teenagers are the target. They are so vulnerable, and in adolescence attitudes are formed that may stay with a person for life. When I first came to this country, people told me that the teenage years are the golden years. I disagree. They are the glandular years – the glands call the tune and set the tempo, too. One reason I feel so tender toward teenagers is that I know how powerful sexual drives can be and how helpless one can be to resist them.

In most parts of India, segregation of the sexes is the norm. But I come from an unusual tradition. In my family boys and girls are together even as teenagers, and this seems very healthy to me. It is good for young people to attend classes together, play together, study together. But I do not think they are ready for sexual relations. To give sex a place in a lasting, loving relationship requires enormous maturity, which even many adults do not have. It requires rare sensitivity, self-forgetfulness, and attention to the other person's needs. To expect teenagers to rise to these heights is cruelly unfair.

I have lived close to hundreds of young people and have taught thousands more, and I can attest from more than fifty years of playing Ann Landers that whenever a relationship is founded on sex, it's just a matter of time

– a few months, sometimes just a few weeks – before it is disrupted. With anguish in their eyes, so many young men and women have come to me and asked, "What is the matter with us? We couldn't bear to be without each other, and now I don't even want to run into him on the street."

I tell them, "There is nothing wrong with you. But your relationship has no foundation. Jesus put it very well when he said a house built on sand cannot last."

If they ask, "What is the lasting foundation on which you can build love?" I tell them, "Put the other person first. Learn to understand her needs, or his needs, as well as you do your own." If they have some depth, they will get very quiet and serious at this point, because putting someone else first is not easy. It's easy to give a gift or write a sonnet, but to put the other person first, you have to reduce your own self-will. When they have grasped what I'm saying, most of my young Romeos and Juliets grin ruefully, shrug their shoulders, and decide they probably aren't ready for romance yet after all. With a sigh of relief they head back to the soccer field or the ballet studio. One-to-one relationships had better wait a few years.

To learn to love takes many years, and even in the twenties it doesn't come easily. But by that time we have at least weathered the most stressful period of emotional and physiological change, and we are ready to start learning. Experience – with luck, not too bitter – has made vividly clear to us certain truths that as teenagers we could only dimly suspect. We've come to realize, probably, that like most people our deepest desire is for permanent, loving relationships. And we've watched ourselves trying in vain to build those relationships on a physical, sexual basis. The physical basis promises so much – it's such a clever salesman. But we've begun to see through the sales pitch, and we're pretty sure now that what it promises it can never deliver.

What draws us again and again into sexual involvement is that for just a moment it releases us from the deep sense of separateness that haunts every human being. In a completely loving and loyal relationship, sex can have a beautiful place, but lasting love is not based on sex. Lasting romance has two precious components: increasing respect, and tenderness that grows every day. This is what all of us want in a relationship. Once we've tasted it and the closeness it brings, we begin to move beyond the physical barrier.

Once a relationship is secure on a lasting foundation, two people who are deeply in love can enter a third stage which brings even more fulfillment: they can begin to work together for a great cause. This is the very flowering of romance. It doesn't bring just the two of them together; it draws them into a loving relationship with many, many others, who come in time to think together as with one mind, to feel together as with one heart, to work together as with a single pair of hands.

In the final stage of romantic love, you come to have a loving relationship with every creature, expressed in whatever way is perfectly suited to each. Your love for your partner has not diminished in the least; it has simply expanded to include all of life. Now you are relating to the Self, who is One in all. And indeed, this final stage is what you've wanted from the first. From there you can look back and see that sexual desire was really the yearning for unity – unity with one person to begin with, but ultimately with all of life.

All of us are given a reasonable margin in our early years to experiment with sex, but it is prudent for us to use our understanding to see what tremendous power it has and how that power can best be used. We should never allow ourselves to get despondent or discouraged. Mahatma Gandhi wanted to take a vow of celibacy, but even he confesses that he had to take it three times. The Compassionate Buddha said that if he had had one more force like sex to reckon with, he would not have made it. If spiritual giants like these found the challenge so formidable, we shouldn't despair.

For harnessing and directing the sex faculty and bringing it under our control, we are given a great instrument: the human will. A German mystic of the early Middle Ages, Gertrude the Great, describes an exchange between herself and the Lord within. "O Lord," she exclaims, "would that I might have a fire that could liquefy my soul, so that I could pour it totally out like a libation unto thee!"

And the Lord replies: "Thy will is such a fire."

If any man love, he knoweth what is the cry of this voice. For it is a loud cry in the ears of God, the mere ardent affection of the soul, when it saith, "My God, my love, thou art all mine, and I am all thine."

Every time you repeat the Holy Name, it is a call for the Lord to reveal himself in your heart. When you use your mantram under great stress – of longing, of fear, even of terrible anger or anxiety – that call is truly "a loud cry" that almost pitches you into the very arms of the Lord. In the latter stages of meditation, when you have been using the mantram with all your might and the Lord doesn't seem to be responding, you'll be calling out with a keen sense of deprivation – and that will make your cry all the louder.

Teresa of Avila was so passionately in love with her Lord that he used to appear before her regularly. He had no choice! Her love was so strong that he belonged to her completely. And, of course, she belonged to him – so utterly that when she took her vows as a Carmelite nun, she ceased to be Teresa de Ahumada y Cepeda, daughter of a proud and titled aristocratic family, and chose the name "Teresa of Jesus."

Once, the story goes, a radiant figure appeared to young Teresa in a vision and asked, "Little one, what is your name?"

"Sir," she replied, "I am Teresa of Jesus" – meaning, "I don't belong to myself at all; I belong completely to

my Lord." Then, taking him to be an angel and pluck-
ing up her courage, Teresa asked, "And who may you
be?"

The radiant figure must have been moved by this
sweet reply, for he smiled and answered, "I am Jesus of
Teresa."

Chapter Ten

*Enlarge thou me in love, that with
the inward palate of my heart I may
taste how sweet it is to love, and to be
  dissolved, and as it were to bathe myself
in thy love.*

*Let me be possessed by love, mounting
above myself through excessive fervor
and admiration.*

*Let me sing the song of love; let me follow
thee, my Beloved, on high; let my soul
spend itself in thy praise, rejoicing through
love.*

When Thomas said, "My God, my love, thou art all
mine, and I am all thine," the courtship period was over,
for two had become one: in the beautiful phrase of John
of the Cross, "*Amada en el amado transformada.*" Now
the lover and the Beloved are singing "the song of love"
together, and their language is reckless. Let me "be *dissolved*" in love, "*possessed* by love; . . . let my soul
spend itself in thy praise." One thinks of Saint Francis
preaching on his tiptoes in ecstasy or playing an imagi-
nary fiddle to accompany a song he alone hears.

The aspirant does not ask, in this passage, that the Lord should love him, but rather that his own capacity to love be enlarged to its utmost. He asks for the supreme experience – that his soul "spend itself in thy praise, rejoicing through love."

Enlarge thou me in love, that with
the inward palate of my heart I may
taste how sweet it is to love, and to be
dissolved, and as it were to bathe myself
in thy love.

Many years ago, when I took a bungalow on the Blue Mountain and went to live there with my mother, one of my uncles came to visit us. Uncle Appa had taught me Shakespeare and opened my eyes to the classics of Western literature. He spent a few days with us and admired the magnificent views down the mountain slopes: the tea plantations, the silver eucalyptus trees, the bright blue sky. He observed the stillness of the hill country and felt how clear and cool the air was at that height. Finally he gave me a warm smile, and with a knowing look he said, "I see now why you wanted this place. You want to write poetry."

There had been a time not too long before when his guess would have been right. My passionate love of nature and my equally passionate love of poetry were really one love. They reinforced each other. And when

I walked those beautiful curving roads on the Blue Mountain, whole passages from Wordsworth would come to mind:

> Five years have past; five summers, with the length
> Of five long winters! and again I hear
> These waters, rolling from their mountain springs
> With a soft inland murmur. – Once again
> Do I behold these steep and lofty cliffs,
> That on a wild secluded scene impress
> Thoughts of more deep seclusion; and connect
> The landscape with the quiet of the sky.

But I had already reached the stage in my life when neither the love of poetry nor of nature – not even the two together – could satisfy me completely. Slowly but surely, my deep love of nature and poetry was being transmuted into an all-consuming love of the Self. A new desire was stirring within me. I wanted, in the words of Thomas a Kempis, to be "enlarged." I wanted to climb "above myself."

Up until that period, I'd have insisted that my life was full and complete. I loved writing; I loved teaching English; and I loved my vacations, too! At the end of the term, right after my last class, the horse carriage would be waiting just outside the classroom with all my luggage aboard. I would jump on it, rush to catch the Grand Trunk Express, and be reunited with my family on the Blue Mountain two days later. My colleagues were very happy to see this. "What devotion to his family!" they would exclaim.

But now that I had begun to meditate, I knew all this was not enough. Mahatma Gandhi's words went right

into my heart when he said that if you don't love everybody on earth, you are not a lover of God. It was not
that I was coming to love my family less, but I was beginning to love those around me equally, because now
my capacity for love was growing. It was all so mysterious to me, so new. A certain creative process had begun
to work in me, and I had no idea what the final result
would be. All I could do was cooperate.

This can happen to every one of us, over a long, long
time. We start with our own family, our partner, our
child, but then gradually we extend the circle of our
compassion and affection to our neighbor. Slowly, it
moves on down the street. In time, our new capacity to
love is so strong that it won't let us ignore the needs of
homeless people on the other side of town. Then it extends to the county, then to the state. This is how it develops, and this is why it takes some years. We can say,
"Oh, this is impossible!" But there is Saint Francis saying, "I have done it," and Saint Teresa saying, "I have
done it." The more we love, the more we *can* love. This
is what it means to enlarge ourselves in love.

The ordinary world of the ego and the senses is so
confining! The pleasures of the palate, for instance, are
so small, for all the energy we put into indulging them.
That is why Thomas cries out to taste with an *"inward
palate . . .* how sweet it is to love." It is very much the
same with music, too. As a young man, Francis of
Assisi had been a great lover of music. He and his
friends would sing and play through the streets of Assisi
late at night. Years later, however, he would describe a
different kind of music – so exquisite that if it had con-

tinued even a second longer, he said, his heart would have broken in two.

My own love of poetry and nature followed much the same course. I loved poetry before – I couldn't get enough of it – but today there is a magnificent poetry woven into every moment. I loved nature before, too, but today my love is so much deeper. It goes beyond how I *feel*. Now I am careful to do nothing that might hurt the environment.

When this fierce desire – to throw off the old limits and become the immense Self you were meant to be – first sets in, there is a lot of anguish in it. I can testify there is both pain and rapture. Your life becomes full of contradictions. It is an unsettling state of affairs, when those old attachments by which you had defined your personality are falling away. But to compensate, when your attraction to external pleasures has weakened, inside you begin to have deep experiences in meditation. Just for a couple of seconds the mind is still. For one minute the ego falls asleep. You feel such a thrill of joy when this happens, and such fullness of love, that now you tell yourself, "Nothing has been lost."

Great mystics have conveyed this in many ways. Saint Augustine writes in the *Confessions* of just such a glimpse, and he recorded the experience in joyous language much like Thomas's: "No further would I read, nor needed I, for instantly, even with the end of this sentence, by a light as it were of confidence now darted into my heart, all the darkness of doubting vanished away."

When Augustine wrote these lines he was a seasoned veteran of the spiritual life, looking back on something

that had happened long before. Decades of spiritual disciplines lay behind him, long years of labor in the service of his Lord. Those years had brought him repeated,
incontrovertible experiences of God's presence within.
But that first moment in a garden in Milan would remain fresh and luminous for him always, as it has for
untold numbers of aspirants who have drawn courage
from his story. No one has described with greater dramatic power the long, painful struggle to turn inward,
and the joy of finally doing so. Even today, the *Confessions* reads like a well-paced, gripping novel – as arresting now as when it was written more than sixteen hundred years ago. I have read it many times, and I am always surprised at how contemporary the story seems,
and how familiar.

Outwardly, Augustine's world bore little resemblance to ours. The pace was slower, quieter. The traffic
certainly moved more slowly. There was no talk of van-
ishing ozone layers or acid rain. Yet hanging over everything was a brooding awareness of inconceivably great
changes about to take place. The vast, all-encompassing
reality, the great Roman Empire, was moribund. Sick at
the center, unwell in every limb, it was dying, and dying
along with it were the state religion and the elaborate
civic mythologies that had shored it up. In its place, extending across the entire Mediterranean world, was a
seething turmoil of competing philosophies, creeds,
and cults. Augustine had left none of these unexamined.
The Christian faith of his birth and upbringing had
seemed too simple, too childlike, to satisfy his fierce
and well-schooled intellect. Yet none of the other teach-

ings he explored seemed to satisfy anything *but* his intellect.

At only thirty-two, Augustine had been appointed official imperial rhetorician for the city of Milan: he had *arrived*. Satisfaction, though, had not. Nothing of what he had been accustomed to enjoy – not his friendships and romantic involvements, not his formidable intellectual achievements or the quiet rewards of teaching – none of it held him any more. None of it could still the questions that haunted him day and night.

The sheer depth of his mother's religious life attracted him now as it never had before. Friends meanwhile were bringing him astonishing reports from Egypt – stories of men and, later, women who were living out the Gospel teachings with apostolic fervor. Saint Anthony was one of these. He was a giant among mystics, who issued this flawless description of deep meditation: "That prayer is perfect when you are no longer aware of who is praying or of the prayer itself."

For Anthony, the moment of truth had come when he was passing by a church where the Gospel was being read. "Go home," he had heard, "and sell all that you have, and come and follow me." The young man in the Gospels had gone away dejected, but Anthony, a successful businessman, had gone straight home to act on Jesus' words. Augustine frankly envied him, as he envied some of his friends, too, who had made what seemed effortless, almost instant transformations of life and will. For the doubts and inhibitions that held Augustine prisoner now were not intellectual but personal. He had tried so many times to reform himself, only to fall back with renewed ardor into his old untrammeled ways. "Lord, give me chastity, but do not give it yet." Augustine can be looked upon as the patron saint of everyone who has ever vacillated on the path to God-consciousness!

At last, tormented after weeks and months of struggle, he hurled himself out of doors one afternoon only half conscious of where he was, and stumbled into the garden of the friend's house where he was staying. Suddenly, from nowhere visible, he heard a child's voice say, "Pick up and read, pick up and read." He rushed to his copy of Saint Paul's Epistles. Could he hope to be as fortunate as Anthony? Would the book speak to him? Opening it, he read the first lines his hand fell upon: "Not in rioting and drunkenness, not in chambering and wantonness, not in strife and envying; but put ye on the Lord Jesus Christ, and make not provision for the flesh, to fulfill the lusts thereof." Not a text that would speak to every one of us, but to Augustine, very much the man-about-town, the wrangling intellectual and ambitious academician, it struck hammer blows. Surely this was the Lord speaking directly to him.

Years later, looking back on that first revelation, Augustine laments in the language of a very personal love, "Too late came I to love thee, O thou Beauty both so ancient and so fresh; yea, too late came I to love thee. And behold, thou wert within me, and I out of myself, where I made search for thee. You were inside, Lord, all the while, and I was looking in all the wrong places."

Down through time, across one generation after another, the *Confessions* has provided a universally recognized pattern for what happens to a human being when he or she turns inward. I, too, felt a shock of recognition when I read Augustine's story. I was just a few years older than Augustine when my own universe began to tilt wildly on its axis. I had established myself as a successful writer and professor of literature. No one had declared me an imperial rhetorician, to be sure, but I *was* head of the campus speech and debate society. I had strong interests in music and drama; I was deeply fond of my students and my work. Yet I, too, had discovered, just beneath the surface satisfaction of it all, a profound sense of insufficiency.

Like Augustine, I had a mother who was deeply established in my ancestral faith. Like him, I had remained outside – skeptical, unconvinced, for all my growing hunger. Meanwhile, the world around me was undergoing unprecedented changes. The vast British Empire that had ruled India for nearly two hundred years was crumbling as surely as Rome's had crumbled, and with it was crumbling the implicit faith I had placed in everything Western. And if Saint Anthony and Saint Ambrose were bright sources of light for Augustine, just so was Mahatma Gandhi for me. His ashram near Nagpur seized my imagination as irresistibly as Saint Anthony's desert enclaves had seized Augustine's.

Saint Augustine wrote vividly about the way old desires crowded about him and tugged at his sleeves; and when I read those lines, I thought he could have been describing my own experience. And I had come up just as hard as he against the utter instability of my mind and will, those sometime friends: "The mind gives an order to the body," he used to say in frustration, "and is at once obeyed. But when it gives an order to itself, it is resisted." Throughout his long and painful struggle, Augustine drew gratefully on his friends for support. But his staunchest spiritual ally, his best friend of all, was without question his mother, Monica. For me it was my grandmother and my mother. It was through their grace, at long last, that I could sing in chorus with Augustine, "Too late came I to love thee, O thou Beauty both so ancient and so fresh . . . "

When people ask me, "Haven't you lost the normal satisfactions of life?" I say, "No! All I have lost is insecurity and inadequacy." I've lost the feeling I was just a plaything of life, without any sense of direction. I feel at home in the world now and comfortable in the universe. I have relationships with all life, and I feel sure this is a romance that will go on life after life. I know that when Saint Francis speaks of Brother Sun and Sister Moon, he is not just being poetic – he is speaking out of a very practical knowledge that beholds the entire world as the manifestation of God's love.

> *. . . that with the inward palate of my heart I may taste how sweet it is to love . . .*

There is a passage in the *Confessions* where Augustine recalls a point early in his own spiritual development when, he says, "I heard thy voice from on high crying unto me: 'I am the food of the full-grown.'" He is referring to one of the first discoveries you will make on the spiritual path. Just as you begin to change your food habits when you start meditation, soon you see that you must change the way you feed your mind as well. Personal pleasure and profit are junk food for the mind. They don't nourish; they don't even satisfy. You still feel hungry afterward. Just as we select food that nourishes the body – fresh, whole foods, foods brimming with nutrients – we learn to do the same for the mind. Kind thoughts, compassionate thoughts, thoughts directed to the welfare of everyone around will be the mainstay of our diet.

When Augustine hears God speaking, he replies in effect, "All right, I won't go on eating in those Carthaginian hot spots – but what *do* I eat?" Then comes the answer, very dramatic, when the Lord says, "And then thou shalt feed on me." Stop eating mindfood that is bad for you, he says, and soon you'll be ravenous. The inspirational passages will look so good!

Augustine wonders, "What'll happen then?" Again the answer comes straight: "Nor shalt thou change me to thy substance. Thou shalt be changed into mine." This is exactly what takes place. The human being becomes a divine force.

After many decades now, meditation is for me a great banquet. In the early hours of the morning, at the holy hour that in India we call *brahmamuhurta*, I get a call from inside saying, "Sit up and meditate! A great banquet is spread for you." Meditation is the nourishing feast that fills my hunger. It is the current that recharges my batteries. It rejuvenates me and heals my wounds.

. . . and to be dissolved . . .

Chemists will tell you there are compounds which resist almost any solvent. I would say that self-will falls into this class. If you put self-will in acids, it'll come right through. Put it in alkalis; it will still be there. *Bury it,* for that matter, and it will grow. There is no simple, fast way to get rid of self-will. But if you can learn over years of effort to put the needs of others first, you will find your self-will beginning to dissolve. When you think more and more about others, it's like applying a super-solvent from within. As you move closer to others, you will move closer to the Lord within, who is your real Self. After many years you actually begin to *lose* yourself in the Lord of Love, and in so doing, you truly find yourself. This transformation is not just spiritual, either; it invades the body and the mind as well. There is a radiance about your appearance, a splendor about your personality, that evokes the deepest response in everybody who is sensitive.

There is no way God can be known to us other than by our becoming part of him. To try to understand the supreme reality we call God through the intellect is like trying to study the sun with a candle. To become lost in him is the highest mode of knowing. Saint Bernard of Clairvaux stated it magnificently:

> Just as a drop of water mixed with wine seems entirely to lose its own identity while it takes on the state of wine and its color; just as iron, heated and glowing, looks very much like fire, having divested itself of the original and characteristic appearance of iron; and just

as air, flooded with the light of the sun, is transformed so that it appears not so much lighted up as to be light itself, so it will inevitably happen that in illumination, every human affection will then, in some ineffable manner, melt away from self and be wholly transformed into the love of God.

When I go deep in meditation, I lose myself in the Lord within and become one in spirit with him. I'm like the little drop of water Bernard describes, and my Boss is a great sea of wine.

. . . and as it were to bathe myself in thy love . . .

In India on a warm, tropical afternoon, there is nothing equal to jumping into a cold river. You are not just in a little tub of water; you become part of the river. Just so, when you see the divine current that flows in the depths of every human being and can keep your eyes on it always, you will be bathing in a river of love.

When I gave classes on the Berkeley campus back in the sixties, there was a loose-limbed Irish setter named Ludwig who used to spend most of his time in the waters of the fountain in front of the Student Union. In fact, Ludwig was something of a mascot, and the fountain was unofficially known as Ludwig's Fountain. We all used to enjoy watching him splash about and throw great plumes of water up to sparkle in the sunlight.

Every one of us, I told my students, has a fountain playing like that in the depths of our consciousness, and we can all take instruction from Ludwig – go there and play and swim and refresh ourselves. The waters of life are not outside; they are right within.

Let me be possessed by love . . .

Don't ever be possessed by *things*. I appreciate everything about modern civilization that makes life comfortable, but if you look carefully, you can see that we are beginning to be possessed by our possessions. The proof is that we feel if we cannot have a particular thing – a particular car, certain clothes, a home computer – we ourselves are incomplete. It is this haunting sense of inadequacy that the media are exploiting, particularly in that interesting phenomenon called "impulse buying." You go to a supermarket to buy a can of cocoa and you come back with a big brown bag full of things. Why? Oh, they were on sale, and they were stacked up right next to the cash register. When things can reach out and compel you to buy them, they have stolen a bit of your capacity to love. That is why the simple life is a very loving life, in which all our precious capacity to love is preserved.

. . . mounting above myself, through excessive fervor and admiration.

Once all your desires are unified, there comes a point in meditation when prayer ceases to have words. The words of the inspirational passage fall away, and your consciousness becomes a field of unified desire which draws you beyond the world of words and thoughts. This is a mysterious state, and it can be frightening to find yourself plunged into its depths. Theophan the Recluse describes it and allays our fears, making it clear that this is a stage all seekers pass through:

> Further on in this state, another kind of prayer may be given which comes to a man instead of being performed by him. . . . The spirit of God comes upon man and drives him into the depths of the heart as if he were taken by the hand and forcibly led from one room to another. The soul is here taken captive by an invading force and is kept willingly within as long as this overwhelming power of prayer still holds sway over it.

This is a perfect description of what happened to me during the deeper stages of meditation. I used to say, "This is enough! I have gone deep enough; I don't want to go any farther." But something kept dragging me down into a deeper place, out into a brighter room.

You, too, may come to a stage where you feel there is a power driving you from behind, drawing you from in front. At that time, because of the depths you have reached in meditation, it is very important to throw yourself into selfless and concentrated work in harmony with others. This is for your own safety. It's important also to eat nourishing food in moderate quantities. Regular, vigorous exercise is important at this time, and so is wholesome entertainment. The body and the nervous system both have to be strengthened to withstand the impact of these tremendous developments.

Gradually, at this stage, meditation will cease to be a discipline. It will become a source of such ravishing joy that there is the danger of wanting to bask in it. This is where you safeguard your progress by making a rich contribution in your outward life. You have inhaled; now you must exhale. You find yourself in possession of joy that never deserts you, for if others are in distress, you have the great joy of being able to relieve their pain. If they are happy, you have the great joy of sharing their happiness. You live in a world of joy. You don't have to go anywhere in search of joy; joy comes in search of you. Saint Anselm of Canterbury describes his own experience: "I have found a joy that is full and more than full. For when heart and mind and soul, and all the man are full of that joy, joy beyond measure will still remain."

Let me sing the song of love . . .

"When your life becomes a song," said a Bengali mystic, "the Lord listens."

Years ago I visited the home of a friend and we were seated on the terrace together. The wind was blowing, and I heard the dulcet tinkling of bells. Looking around, I saw there were wind chimes which were making sweet music out of the wind. I could well imagine a storm coming and the music becoming even sweeter – a hurricane, and the music becoming a kind of symphony. The lover of God lives very much like the wind chime. When joy comes, he sings a sweet refrain; but when sorrow comes, oh! the song becomes sweeter; and when great trials come, tremendous hymns burst forth from his consciousness.

The Greek philosopher Plotinus loved to talk about human consciousness using this same language of music. "We are like a chorus," he said, "who stand around the conductor but do not always sing in tune because our attention is diverted by looking at external things."

Imagine the London Philharmonic Orchestra in one of those outside theaters, performing under the direction of a great conductor. What would you think if the members of the wind section kept gazing out into the audience while the violinists followed the planes overhead and the percussionists kept falling asleep? You'd want your money back. "There is no music here," you'd tell the gentleman at the ticket office. "There is no *orchestra* here! Everybody is doing his own thing." Plotinus says we are all living like that, unaware of the divine conductor within.

"But when we do behold him," Plotinus adds, "we attain the end of our existence and our rest. Then we no longer sing out of tune, but form a truly divine chorus about him. In that chorus the soul beholds the fountain of life, the fountain of creativity, the principle of being, the cause of good, and the root of the soul." I cannot express to you in words what this divine harmony is like. There is not a discordant note anywhere, not even in the unconscious. The symphony goes on playing even in sleep.

Let me follow thee, my Beloved, on high . . .

Just as on a high mountain there is a timberline beyond which no trees can grow, so there is a point in consciousness beyond which no thoughts can grow, no selfish desires can take root. We may think, "Who wants to live at an elevation where there is no thought? No cravings to brighten our lives?" But those who climb to that point and come down for our benefit say, "Oh, but the air is like champagne there. You have no idea how it goes to your head! The view will take your breath away. Absolute truth can be seen, and absolute beauty too."

Mountain climbers train to climb the Himalayas for many, many years. Meditators, similarly, train for decades to climb the Himalayas of the soul. When they stand at the peak and look around, they say: "The world is full of God! I see now that in everyone there is the divine. There is a continuing relationship between mountain and sea, forest and river, and all living things."

Don't be content to climb only the Sierras or the Alps. As Saint Augustine said, that is not enough: "People travel afar to marvel at the heights of mountains, the mighty waves of the sea, the long courses of great rivers, the vastness of the ocean, the movements of the stars, yet they leave themselves unnoticed!"

Let my soul spend itself in thy praise,
rejoicing through love.

Before I took to meditation, I had no idea what wealth I had locked up in my heart. I was like someone spending out of a checking account, watching anxiously each month as "Checks Written" overtook "Cash in Balance," completely unaware that in the depths of my consciousness there was a great savings account that I could draw on, a vast trust fund in my name. After many years I was finally able to go deep in meditation and unlock this treasury. Then I discovered how rich I was, and with that discovery came the immediate, passionate desire to lay hold of that vast wealth of love, wisdom, and resourcefulness and pour it out at the feet of the Lord.

Chapter Eleven

Let me love thee more than myself, nor love myself but for thee: and in thee all that truly love thee, as the law of love commandeth, shining out from thyself.

Just as the law of relativity can be verified in England or in Japan by English or Japanese physicists, the law of love that Thomas expresses in these verses can be verified by lovers of God both East and West. Reading selections from Meister Eckhart, for example, is almost like reading selections from the South Indian mystic Shankara Acharya. In fact, since *meister* and *acharya* signify the same thing, we can as well say "Meister Shankara" and "Eckhart Acharya," so deep do the similarities go. Similarly, there are two marvelous women mystics, one from India and one from Europe, who sing of the love of God and dance in ecstasy to express their love of God; and when translated into the language of the heart, there is no difference between Mechthild of Magdeburg and Meera of Rajasthan.

About three hundred years separate them. Meera was born around 1498; Mechthild, between 1207 and 1210. Meera shed her body before she was fifty; Mechthild lived to be eighty or more. Both of them adopted the rich devices of courtly love poetry to compose their songs for the Lord within, and the similarities between the two are remarkable.

Meera was born a royal princess of the Rajput people. Her menfolk were brave warriors who fought the Mogul emperor in Delhi. She herself grew up cherished and protected, in an atmosphere of music and dance; but as her spiritual life deepened, she displayed the courage of the Rajputs more brilliantly than her most formidable uncles and brothers.

When Meera was just a little girl, she received an image of Lord Krishna from a wandering teacher who saw great spiritual promise in the girl, and from that day onwards she felt she was betrothed to Krishna. In accordance with the customs of her people, she was married at about eighteen to a prince from a nearby state. For years she struggled to fulfill her new family's expectations of her and still remain the passionate devotee of Krishna that she couldn't help but be. At last, after she had survived three attempts on her life and innumerable assaults to her spiritual life, she answered the call of her first and only love. Carrying nothing with her but her vina, the stringed instrument with which she accompanied her songs, she walked out of her royal palace and never came back. For the rest of her days she wandered through northwest India composing love songs to Lord Krishna – songs which are sung throughout India even today. Legend has it that as Meera was singing in a Krishna temple one day, her longing for him reached such a height that before her companions' eyes she simply vanished into the figure of her divine beloved.

About Mechthild's childhood we know very little, but her poems suggest that she too was brought up in a courtly setting. When she was about twelve she had her first spiritual experience, a "greeting" from Christ that was so powerful that afterward the worldly life never exerted any real pull. At twenty-three she left her family and moved to the town of Magdeburg, bent on severing any attachment that might hinder her pursuit of the Lord within. Mechthild's native state of Thuringia was in a period of spiritual awakening then, and Magdeburg was a place where women seekers in particular were coming together in loosely-bound spiritual communities within a lay movement known as the Beguines. Mechthild lived in Magdeburg as a Beguine until she was an elderly woman. In 1270 she went to live in the famous convent of Helfta, where she died in 1297.

Mechthild drew upon the richness of chivalric poetry to express her love of God. Mostly she just scribbled her songs on pieces of paper that were not collected until much later. By 1300, however, Mechthild's songs were being circulated around Europe, and tradition has it that when Dante wrote his *Divine Comedy,* it was she the great poet was describing when he wrote of "a solitary woman moving, singing, and gathering up flower on flower – the flowers that colored all her pathway." It is a beautiful image, and one very much in the spirit of Meera too, for it suggests that the lives of those who dedicate themselves to the service of God are not austere at all. They are lives strewn with flowers, full of joy, full of love.

Let me love thee more than myself, nor
love myself but for thee . . .

Meera writes, in vivid images drawn from everyday life:

> None can break the bond between you and me,
> none but you, O Lord of the world.
> You are the tree, Krishna,
> and I the bird that sits on the branches singing.
> You are the river, Krishna,
> and I the fish that swims in joy
> from bank to bank.
> You are the green hill, Krishna,
> and I the peacock dancing,
> with flashing plumes spread.
> Accept Meera's devotion, Lord of the world!

Mechthild's intimate tone echoes Meera's:

> Thou shinest in my soul
> As the sun on gold.
> When I rest in thee, O Lord,
> My bliss is manifold.
> Thou clothest thyself with my soul
> Who thyself art its mantle.

Both these great mystics appeal to their Lord in irresistibly sweet language. Meera teases, "Some people say I flirted with you, others that I cheated you, but I got you, Krishna!" And Mechthild sings just as playfully:

> I seek thee with all my might.
> Had I the power of a giant thou wouldst quickly
>   be lost
> If I came upon thy footprints.

> Ah, my love, run not so far ahead,
> But rest a little lovingly
> That I may catch up with thee!

And both of them rise to the very heights of poetry when they describe their longing for permanent union with the Beloved. From Mechthild:

> Even should all creatures lament for me,
> none could fully tell them
> what inhuman need I suffer.
> Human death were far gentler to me
> than to be without you.
> I seek thee in my thoughts
> like a bride seeking a groom.

And from Meera:

> In life and death you are my friend,
> My only friend.
> Without your presence
> I am lost in the maze of life.
> Ask my heart and it will tell you
> Whose face it is seeking always.
> This world is but a shadow play
> Where family and friends flit by.
> I pray to you with folded hands
> And beg you to heed my prayer.

Mechthild and Meera are adamant: if you want to be united with the Lord, there can't be anything else you want more. There comes a point in every great mystic's life when he or she is put to the test: nothing can be held back. Mechthild reveals on one occasion that God actually said to her, "To have all that mine is, you must let go of all that thine is." And in one of the most precious of all Hindu scriptures, the Bhagavatam, there is a verse that has inspired people like me down the ages all over India. It is very much in keeping with these lines from Thomas a Kempis, because it contains the supreme secret of devotion. "If you want to be united with me," the Lord says, "you must lay hold on whatever it is in life that gives you most delight – whatever it is you think you cannot live without – and give it to me. Infinite are the blessings that will follow."

To make this gift – to look about you and find what gives you most satisfaction in life and say, "Here, Lord, it's yours!" – is next to impossible. For my own part, I can attest that I was in love with my work and in love with life as I was living it then. My students were dear to me, and I to them. That was my whole world. All my attention had been flowing into it, and I would never have been able to imagine that I could live without it.

But as your need for the Lord within – call him Christ or Krishna, call her the Divine Mother – as that need becomes more and more imperious, circumstances start to change. If you were to ask me how I was able to give up a career and way of life I loved so much, I would have to say that it wasn't through my own effort at all. It was through my grandmother's grace that everything changed in such a way that if I hadn't voluntarily let go, it would probably have been taken from me anyway. That kind of divine banditry is considered to be one of the highest forms of grace.

Mechthild describes in magnificent poetry her own response when from deep within she heard the divine voice say, "Hand it over!" God says:

> "Thou huntest so for thy love.
> What bringest thou me, my queen?"

> "Lord, I bring thee my treasure.
> It is greater than the mountains,
> wider than the world,
> deeper than the sea,
> higher than the clouds,
> more glorious than the sun,
> more manifold than the stars.
> It outweighs the whole earth."

The Lord lets her know he's interested, and asks:

> "What is the name of thy treasure?"

And the soul replies:

> "Lord, it is called my heart's desire.
> I have withdrawn it from the world,
> denied it to myself and all creatures.
> Now I can bear its weight no longer.
> Where, O Lord, shall I lay it?"

The Lord is so pleased that he opens his arms to her and bids her come:

> "Nowhere shalt thou lay it
> But in my own divine heart
> and on my human breast.
> There alone wilt thou find comfort
> And be embraced by my holy spirit."

Mechthild has set aside everything in her life that could have separated her from her Beloved, and now she is lost in union with him. This is what mystics of every spiritual tradition call the Divine Marriage, and in their passionate descriptions of this state they call forth the romantic in each of us. Henry Suso, who lived just a hundred years later than Mechthild, writes ingenuously: "I will set down here a short description how it is when the Bride thus embraces the Bridegroom, for the consideration of the reader, who perhaps has not yet been in this wedding chamber. It may be he will be desirous to follow."

And that is just how it is. Each of us, Suso suggests, approaches the spiritual life at our own pace. Few rush right into this marriage. Instead, first, we get an invitation. It seems innocent enough: "Please come and help us celebrate." We go and sit at the back and look around. Maybe we even attend the reception, and have a couple of glasses of champagne and a piece of cake. That is how we begin. The next time we come as a friend of the bride's. We get a good seat in the third row, and as the bride and bridegroom come down the aisle they look at us and we manage to give them a warm glance in return. Then, as chance would have it, at the next wedding we find ourselves standing right up there next to the altar as a bridesmaid or a best man. It doesn't seem like a bad idea at all! And finally, the great day comes when we are there as the bride or bridegroom. The ceremony passes, we exchange rings, and at last, in a symbolic gesture with universal meaning, we lift the veil and gaze into the eyes of our Beloved.

In the words of Meister Eckhart, "As long as the soul has not thrown off all her veils, however thin, she is unable to see God. Any medium, even a hair's breadth, between the body and the soul stops the actual union." In Sufism, the mystical tradition of Islam, it is said that with every stage in deepening meditation, you remove one veil. The lover, the spiritual aspirant, is yearning to see his divine Beloved, who is heavily veiled. One veil falls away – the physical – and you can see the Self a little more clearly. The mental veil falls away and you see more clearly still. Finally, when the ego falls – the veil of self-will – there is the Beloved, revealed in all the beauty and all the love we have been longing for.

One Sufi poet used to ask, "Do you know why God is veiled from you? Would you like to know what the veil is?" We all say, "Of course!" And he replies, "You yourself are the veil. If you remove your self, you will be able to love all." Our modern civilization says just the opposite: "Thicken the veil! Make it opaque! Wear many layers piled on top of one another!" As a result, not only can no one see us, we cannot see either. Love is not blind, you know; love *sees*. "Love hath no errors." Only when you love can you see everybody's needs.

It's a wonderful paradox: it is when you have seen God in your own heart, in the depths of meditation, that you see him everywhere, even with your eyes wide open. In the great climax of meditation, when self-will is extinguished and the mind becomes still, you see the whole universe as the manifestation of God's love. You love everybody now because you see the Self in them, and not only human beings but animals too – elephants, sea lions, sparrows, every living thing. Wherever you go, you'll see only unity. You will find the universe friendly. For me it is one world, in which not only are all human beings part of my family, so are the seas, the mountains, the rivers, the trees. After all, it isn't governments and corporations that supply me with oxygen; it is plants and plankton. They are my dearest friends, my kith and kin. This is the ultimate reach of the supreme marriage that takes place deep in meditation: I am joined in marriage to all of life.

At weddings in North India, it is customary to apply distilled rose water to the wrist of each guest. It is so fragrant and lasts so long that wherever you go afterward, people will smile and say, "Hey, you must have come from a wedding!" Just so, the Buddha says, when you meet a lover of God, you take a little of that fragrance home in your heart. You will be more patient, more understanding, more secure, more selfless. That is why people loved to be around saints like Francis of Assisi and Teresa of Avila. We instinctively seek the company of men and women like this, and when we find them, we feel so comfortable – not even talking, just being nearby. Once you have begun to meditate, you will find this taking place in your own home. A kind of quietly healing influence can be felt wherever there is even one person whose mind is at peace and whose heart is full of love.

> *. . . and in thee, all that truly love thee . . .*

In the eleventh century, Saint Anselm composed a beautiful prayer in which he asks the Lord, "Teach me to seek thee, and reveal thyself to me when I seek thee; for I cannot seek thee except thou teachest me, nor find thee except thou revealest thyself."

Often God reveals himself through the men and women who love him with all their heart. If you ask any illumined teacher from the Hindu tradition what is the best way to deepen your love for God, he or she will reply, "Through the company of those who have realized God." This is the unspoken, powerful attraction that men like Francis of Assisi and Meister Eckhart exerted on those around them in medieval Europe, and this is why people sought out Julian of Norwich and Catherine of Genoa for spiritual counsel.

There is no equivalent to the highly personal and intimate communication that goes on between an earnest seeker and a realized man or woman. In my own life, without knowing why, I began early to seek out such people. I didn't try to talk with them; it was enough just to look at them.

It began when I was a graduate student at the University of Nagpur, when every weekend I used to love to visit the railway station. Nagpur is located at a crossroads between north and south, east and west, and the great trains from all parts of India came through. I would wait on the platform, and sooner or later most of the important political figures would pass by. And one of them, like Gandhi, was much, much more than just a political figure. Badshah Khan was a great man of God, and although he came from a Muslim race that is one of the fiercest on earth – the Pathans, of the mountainous regions around the Khyber Pass – he had become so ardent a devotee of nonviolence that we called him the

Frontier Gandhi. He was so tall that he had to stoop to come out of the train. His laughter and speech were like sweet music – so gentle coming from such a huge mountain of a man! It was from those encounters on the railway platform that I received from him the inspiration to write his life's story, *A Man to Match His Mountains*, many years later.

There were more of these precious encounters with spiritual figures, and each of them came without any effort on my part. Through one of my campus colleagues I was privileged to meet Meher Baba. Much later another friend took me and Christine to the ashram of Swami Ramdas, where we sat and watched him looking like the most ordinary fellow in the world as he shaved himself and fiddled with the dial on his radio to get the morning news.

Soon afterwards, when Christine and I were visiting Vrindavan, the place where the historic Krishna lived, I learned by happenstance that a beautiful woman saint named Anandamayi Ma was there in her ashram that day and accepting visitors. I ran back to get Christine, and we arrived just in time. There was quite a large crowd. I remember several Indian visitors trying to touch Anandamayi Ma's feet, which is our way of paying deep respect. She prohibited them gently, directing each of them to her mother as if to say, "It is her feet you should touch, not mine; for it was she who brought me into this life." As we were leaving, this gracious and saintly woman took a garland from her own neck and put it around Christine's.

From all of these encounters, I have drawn a precious and rare kind of sustenance. I call them my "teachers at large," for each of them transmitted to me a glimmering of my own deepest Self. But most powerful of all, and most telling for the whole course of my life, was my meeting with Gandhi.

Those were critical years in India's struggle for independence from British rule, when terrible problems confronted the country. I yearned to have a part in solving them, but I was very young, and it was impossible for me not to feel overwhelmed. In search of guidance, I made a kind of pilgrimage one day to Gandhi's ashram, outside a town called Wardha. I walked the six or seven miles from the railroad station, and when I arrived I found that a crowd had gathered around the little cottage where Gandhi had been meeting with his co-workers for several hours. I felt sure he would be fatigued when he appeared, that his step would be dragging and the last thing he would want to see was a crowd of people. But when the door opened and Gandhi stepped out, he looked as bright and vital as someone who'd slept eight hours. "Come on," he gestured at us, and he set out walking at a clip that soon had most of us panting. For a moment – just an instant – our eyes met. That is all I was conscious of at the time, just a look. But many years later I began to understand that in a deep, mysterious way, that look continued to give me strength. I realized that a wordless communication must have taken place, though I didn't know how to decode it at the time and had to keep it "pending" until much later.

... as the law of love commandeth, shining out from thyself.

One of the first and most eloquent opponents of slavery in this country was the Quaker, John Woolman, who deeply loved *The Imitation of Christ.* Here is his own testimony to the "law of love":

> There is a principle which is pure, placed in the human mind, which in different places and ages hath had different names. It is, however, pure and proceeds from God. It is deep, and inward, confined to no forms of religion, nor excluded from any, where the heart stands in perfect sincerity. In whomsoever this takes root and grows, of what nation soever, they become brethren in the best sense of the expression.

> God has given us several laws. The law of gravity is a divine gift; and so is the law of unity. We have discovered the one, but not the other. The law of gravity governs the external world; the law of unity governs the internal world. Just as all the planets and all the galaxies are held together in an immense unity by gravitational forces, human beings also, the mystics say, are held together by the law of unity – beginning with the members of the family and extending to all other families, beginning with one nation and extending to all other nations.

> These are not pious platitudes; they are living laws. It is because we have broken them that there is war, there is famine, there is hostility between man and woman, child and parent, friend and friend. But whenever we

see a person who has patience, we are seeing that law of love shining through. The love of the Lord, the glory of the Lord, shines out through every human being to the extent that he is able to bless them that curse him, that she does good to those who harm her. It starts with each one of us.

Chapter Twelve

Love is active, sincere, affectionate, pleasant, and amiable; courageous, patient, faithful, prudent, long-suffering, manly, and never seeking itself.

For in whatever instance a person seeketh himself, there he falleth from love.

Love is circumspect, humble, and upright; not yielding to softness or to levity, nor attending to vain things; it is sober, chaste, steady, quiet, and guarded in all the senses.

Love is subject and obedient to its superiors, to itself mean and despised, unto God devout and thankful, trusting and hoping always in him, even then when God imparteth no relish of sweetness unto it: for without sorrow none liveth in love.

*He that is not prepared to suffer all things,
and to stand to the will of his Beloved, is
not worthy to be called a lover of God.*

*A lover ought to embrace willingly all that
is hard and distasteful for the sake of his
Beloved, and not to turn away from him
for any contrary accidents.*

The fruit of the spirit, said Saint Paul, "is love, joy, peace, long-suffering, gentleness, goodness, faith, meekness, temperance; against such there is no law." In other words, these are the real qualities of the Self. For the great majority of us they are hidden and weighed down by masses of self-will, but at the first opportunity they will rise from below the surface level of consciousness.

This is one of the thrilling developments in deepening meditation. Your mind has not yet become completely still, but it is certainly quieter, and as the turbulence dies down, you begin to see wonderful qualities rising from deep within. Gradually – *gracefully* – they will come into play in your daily life. It is really very much like watching a plum tree or a peach tree bursting into blossom. When somebody is angry at you, the desire to help that person will thrust aside your own angry replies, because you will feel the pain of the other person's anger and want to relieve it. When somebody is being rather obnoxious and your normal desire would be to move away, you will find yourself trying to move closer instead.

In the Indian tradition, the symbol for this wonderful development is the lotus. One of its Sanskrit epithets is *pankaja,* from the word *panka,* "mud," and *ja,* "born." The lotus is born in the mud at the bottom of a lake and finds its way up through the waters until it reaches the surface, where it extends its rosy petals like a chalice of light in the rays of the morning sun. Similarly, even though our capacity to love is born in selfishness and a few strong personal attachments to people near us, it can slowly begin to rise, through the practice of spiritual disciplines, moving upward through the waters of life. You begin by loving A, B, or C, but you end by becoming love itself.

Mystics who use the language of spiritual courtship to describe their experience will often refer to the later stages of meditation as a kind of "holy fecundity." It is the mystics' capacity to bring goodness into the world, whatever their context. In Jesus' own words, "By their fruits ye shall know them."

Teresa of Avila, for example, who felt herself to be a bride of Christ, makes a careful distinction between the honeymoon and the marriage itself. For some time after she first attained spiritual awareness, she was subject to sudden raptures – *arrobamientos* – which would sweep her without warning into the embrace of the Lord within, and altogether *out of* everyday existence. Over time, however, people close to her observed that she was no longer subject to these spells, and they asked her whether she missed them. Teresa smiled and said no: "I've found a better way to pray." She had moved out of the honeymoon stage, and now all the fire and passion of those earlier experiences had come under her conscious control. She could pour her love uninhibitedly into the Lord's work.

Sometimes we are disconcerted to learn that mystics don't live happily ever after. They don't seek to. They ask only to be united with God, even in suffering, and to be instruments of his love.

Let us now touch upon each of the precious qualities Thomas attributes to the man or woman of God:

Love is active . . .

My granny was active all her life. If there was a great feast, she didn't just call the young girls and say, "You do the work." She said, "Help me," and seated together they would slice great piles of okra, eggplant, and green beans – enough for our whole joint family, which numbered about a hundred people. Slowly, one by one, the girls would say, "Granny, I'm falling asleep!" And she would smile and say, "Go to bed then." Toward the end she might be seated there alone, chopping and slicing until daybreak. When my mother would come and ask, "Wouldn't you like to sleep now?" Granny would reply, "Isn't it time to go to the temple?" And that would be the beginning of another day.

In a village society that expected an aristocratic family like mine to rely on servants, my granny really stood out. "She milks her own cows!" people would say. And she could have had the cowherd do it. More than that, when necessary she would clean the cowshed with her own hands. When I asked her, "Granny, why don't you let Appu do it?" She told me, "The cows give us milk. They help take care of us; shouldn't I help take care of them?" She also enjoyed a pithy Kerala saying: "Your own gums are better than somebody else's teeth." She was always independent; and she liked hard work.

Sometimes there is a misconception about the spiritual person: an image of someone who is nice enough, but who doesn't get much done. This couldn't be farther from the truth. When you meditate deeply, you get into danger if you just stop acting. You *need* meaningful, engaging work, work that adds to the benefit of all. When you have gone a little way in meditation, instead of rushing about doing a myriad different things, you learn to act efficiently in ways that are harmonious with your goal; you don't waste time and energy on meaningless activity. You become very active, but in a controlled, focused way. This compatibility of action and contemplation is one of the little known secrets of the meditative life.

. . . *sincere, affectionate, pleasant* . . .

Bernard Shaw said that if you want to judge a person's character, watch him or her in a quarrel. It's a penetrating remark. Do unkind words shoot out of his mouth?

Do unkind things fly from her hand? Similarly, when I want to know how someone is doing in meditation, I just observe that person when he or she is provoked. For just as a ship is tested in a storm, so your spiritual awareness is really tested when anger builds up around you, just daring you to function freely in the emotional turmoil. If you are able to use courteous, kind, considerate language in the midst of towering waves of resentment, your meditation gets A-plus.

Being sincere, affectionate, and pleasant takes a lot of inner toughness. We don't usually associate affection with strength, but there is a very close connection. When it comes to tender, loving relationships, candlelight dinners are fine; but if you want to see whether two people are truly in love, watch them when one is angry. If they're in love, the other should be able to calm that person down; that is one of the "wonderful effects of divine love." Furious words may be flying about your ears, but you just stand there foursquare to all the winds that blow. Such a person is firm, like a mountain or a rock. You remember that Jesus said of Peter, whose name means "rock" in Greek, "Thou art Peter, and upon this rock I shall build my church." For building homes, too, this kind of rock makes the best foundation. When even one member of a household has the security that comes of deep meditation, the house can stand firm. When the storms are blowing, instead of moving away, the lovers will move closer. When danger threatens there won't be two; there will be just one.

For lovers who would reach this state, the precious secret is to cultivate what I call a slow mind. When you learn to meditate, you are slowly shifting the mind from overdrive down to high, then to second, and finally into neutral. Then you have unlimited patience. When someone is angry with you, you can listen to his point of view with such detachment and attention that sometimes you'll say, "Hey, he's right – I'm wrong. I can learn from him."

When I first came to this country, I picked up an apt simile from the laundromat. These machines were so new to me that I watched them with fascination. When you first put your clothes into a dryer, I observed, they whirl around so fast that you can't make out anything; you can't tell your shirt from your socks from your pajamas. But as the machine is about to stop, it slows down. Then you can even read the writing on your T-shirt: "Only Elephants Should Wear Ivory." Similarly, I told my new American friends, when thoughts slow down, we can see them clearly and set them right.

Our best defense against the fast thinking that plunges us into anger is the Holy Name – particularly when it is combined with a really fast walk. In India, some of these essential strategies of the spiritual life are handed out with a delightfully light touch in a little story. One such story concerns a wandering sage who was asked by a villager what to do about anger. "That's simple," the sage said. "Whenever you get angry, just get outside and walk as fast as you can, repeating to yourself the Holy Name: *Rama, Rama, Rama.*" Time passed, and it was months before the sage's wanderings led him to that village again. His villager disciple ran to greet him, but the sage could hardly recognize him. He looked calm and secure but exceptionally fit as well, strong and bronzed by the sun. "I'm glad to see you looking so well!" the sage exclaimed. "What is the secret of your good health?" "Oh," the man answered with an embarrassed smile, "I've been living mostly in the open."

. . . *and amiable* . . .

One of the finest exercises in making your life a work of art is not to regard anybody as an enemy. This can be exceedingly hard. Most people are basically good, but there are some rare individuals, perhaps because of their past, who just can't help returning unkindness for kindness. If you have to deal with them every day – they may even be part of your family! – it can be almost more than you can bear.

The miracle of meditation is that in the long run, even if somebody is unkind to you, you can still return kindness. Even if somebody tries to pull you down, you can pull him up by returning good for evil: blessing those that curse you, in Jesus' words, and doing good to those who hate you. In India, the symbol for this precious capacity is the sandalwood tree. The great mystic Shankara explained why in a haunting poem:

> I have visited many countries,
> Seen many sights,
> But never have I seen anything
> Like the sandalwood tree.
> The more you cut it,

The more you burn it,
The more you grind it,
The more fragrance its hoarded sap will yield.

This is a perfect description of Mahatma Gandhi or Teresa of Avila. The more they were attacked and libeled, the more radiant they became with love. In order to love, we have to learn to suffer. To me, this is the message of Jesus. In our own century, it is Mahatma Gandhi who showed us that love is the sure remedy for even the greatest of evils, war. "Nonviolence," he claimed, "in its dynamic condition, means conscious suffering. It does not mean submission to the will of the tyrant, but it means the pitting of one's whole soul against the will of the tyrant. Working under this law of our being, this 'soul-force,' it is possible for a single individual to defy the whole might of an unjust empire."

. . . *courageous* . . .

"Perfect love," said Saint John, "casteth out fear." Courage is a quality that follows deepening meditation. It implies complete faith in God, whom you *know* to be present in the depths of your consciousness.

Saint Francis of Assisi lived for some time among the people of his region who had contracted leprosy. He bathed them, nursed their wounds, and did everything in his power to relieve their suffering. But to his nearest followers he confided how much resistance in himself he had had to overcome before he could do this. For as a young man, before he was drawn to God, he had been unwilling to go even within miles of the leper houses, and even then he would cover his nostrils in repugnance. But one day – when, in one chronicler's words, "he was beginning to think of holy and useful things" – a leper approached him and stretched out his disfigured hand for alms. Francis tossed him some coins and turned away, revolted to the point of nausea. But then he seems to have seen suddenly that it was Jesus who asked, Jesus in a leper's flesh; and "made stronger than himself," in one of the great understatements of hagiography, he ran back to the man and kissed him in great joy. In that moment of recognition, that sure instinct that the Lord dwells in all, Francis overcame his fear and his repugnance forever.

Courage isn't just something that happens in the lives of the saints and martyrs. The vicissitudes of everyday relationships can call forth enormous courage in every one of us, once we determine to act in the deepest interest of everyone around. For example, putting others first does not mean saying yes to everyone. Love often expresses itself in saying no. When you allow people to exploit you, you aren't just hurting yourself; you are helping the exploiter to hurt himself as well. It requires enormous judgment, and bravery too, to oppose nonviolently people we love – to fight the sin but not the sinner. In time, we can lovingly wear them down with our patience, and when we see signs of regret and reconciliation, we make friends again and completely forget the barrier that stood between us.

To give an example, when I was coming to this country from India, I traveled by ship with many other

Fulbright scholars – including some from Pakistan, whose relations with India were strained to the brink of war. At the dining table, these fellows would try to take it out on me as if I were the prime minister. "Why does your country do this?" they would ask in angry tones. I said, "I'm a plain professor; what do I have to do with setting foreign policy?" But they kept making unpleasant cracks, meal after meal, until the other Indian scholars finally just went to another table.

Now, before I had taken to meditation, I confess I would have done the same. I have never cared for controversy, and there seemed to be nothing gained by staying and arguing. But now I was secure. It was not that I didn't understand their cracks or that their open animosity wasn't painful, but I refused to give them the satisfaction of driving me out. I was convinced that differences in our political opinions need not stand between us as human beings. They kept on baiting me, but I never replied – and I never lost my courtesy, either. This went on almost until we reached Marseilles. There we parted company: they were going on to Gibraltar; I disembarked to take the train for Paris. And the interesting thing was that just as I was leaving, they gave me a party. It was a deeply human response. They were really embarrassed, and with simple courtesy they asked, "Please forgive us for what we have said."

The lovers of God don't play Pollyanna. They don't bury their heads in the sand and say, "Oh, everybody is good; everybody is loving" – not at all. They know the world is a harsh place, and the times we live in are difficult and dangerous. But they have enough security, endurance, and love to remember that all these upsets are on the surface. Beneath the anger and agitation, through every human being a river of love still runs.

. . . patient . . .

The spiritual life calls upon us to be both patient and impatient. Without a certain measure of impatience, you're not likely to cut through all the million and one fetters that tie you to limited, self-willed living. I was as impatient as any of you in the first half of my spiritual life, almost reckless in throwing aside whatever looked like an impediment to becoming aware of God. But in the second half I came to realize that the results of my efforts weren't in my hands at all. Even to have come as far as I had was due entirely to the grace of God. You could say that I became more patient at that point, in that I was more willing just to give full effort and let things take their course. Even so, there was a lot of impatience in the second half, and a lot of suffering too. As Gandhi says, the nearer you are to the goal, the further away it appears to be.

After a retreat last spring, when the participants were taking leave of me, one man lingered until the very last minute and then came to me, gave me a hug, and said, "You have stolen my heart; why can't you steal my mind?" It was a beautiful question, because it expressed so tenderly the mix of patience and impatience that everybody comes to feel on the spiritual path.

. . . faithful . . .

To our modern world, the word *faith* is highly suspect. It seems to imply a lack of intellect, almost a naive gullibility. But every one of us acts on faith every day of our lives. When we get into a car, we put our faith in everybody else on the freeway not to drive into us; we put our faith in the company that built our car, the mechanic who has repaired it, even the engineers who designed the highway. This isn't to say that our faith is unquestioning: we try to be alert when we're behind the wheel, and we choose our mechanic carefully. But once we have done our part, we are willing to trust the car and the roads to get us where we are going in one piece.

This is all the faith I have ever asked anyone to place in God: the same faith you put in your car. You should feel free to place in the Lord who has created the world at least as much faith as you put in the state highway department.

The Hindu scriptures make a bold statement about faith: "You *are* what your faith is." If you believe money will make you happy, you will go after money. If you are convinced fame will make you secure, you will court fame. Why? because in the words of the Bible, "As a person thinketh in his heart, so is he." Not "as a person thinketh in his head," for these beliefs come from a much deeper level than the intellect. In the Orthodox tradition, they say whatever spiritual knowledge you have in the head doesn't become real until you bring it down into the heart through spiritual disciplines. Because of the tremendous distance, this takes many, many years.

. . . *prudent* . . .

There may come moments in meditation when extraordinary experiences take place, and you will be tempted to let your mind soar and bask in the wonder of it all. But every good spiritual teacher will tell you to pay no attention to these occurrences. They have nothing to do with indicating the quality of your meditation, and if you start pursuing them, you can get lost in a kind of Alice's Wonderland of the mind – which, of course, is just what the mind wants you to do!

The real test of deepening meditation is not in the visions we see or voices we hear, but in our capacity to really see the faces of those around us and really hear their voices. Were you able to look through a teenage mask of stony indifference this morning and see the deep yearning for respect and affection it concealed? Did you reach out in love? If so, your meditation is coming along splendidly, no matter how uneventful it might seem.

If by chance you do experience something out of the ordinary – if Saint Teresa should whisper a loving word or two in Spanish as you are falling asleep, or Saint Francis and his sparrows should turn up in a dream – do not dwell upon the experience or become elated. You will only lose the benefit.

Chapter Twelve

. . . long-suffering . . .

A better contemporary translation for this word "long-suffering" would be "enduring." Those who are spiritually aware have an almost endless capacity to endure hardship, mostly because all their attention is given over to the hardships of others. They scarcely notice their own pain and suffering because they are doing everything they can to relieve the suffering of others.

My grandmother demonstrated this marvelous capacity throughout her life. There was one occasion when a painful growth had developed on her back – a carbuncle, I think – and my mother called in a surgeon to remove it. The physician wanted to give Granny an anesthetic, but she insisted it wasn't necessary. She lay down and he performed the surgery, but he was terribly distressed to see that tears were running down her cheeks. "I told you it would hurt!" he said. "Why didn't you take the anesthetic?" Granny just shook her head. "I'm not crying because of the pain," she said in a low voice. "I'm crying because my daughter is crying." My aunts still tell this story because it captures Granny's stature and her sweetness, as well as the tender bond between her and my mother.

... *manly* ...

I would add, of course, "womanly." I come from a matriarchal society, one of the rarest societies in the world, where men and women are called upon not to compete with each other but to complete each other. Most of the men in my family really look upon our women as better guides to life than we men are. My spiritual teacher was my grandmother, and my mother was her teaching aide. I used to consult with girl cousins who were no older than I, because I respected the quiet wisdom they could bring to any question I might have.

The Hindu tradition has passed down a magnificent figure for worship which conveys the cherished ideal of completion between man and woman. God is represented in this figure as half masculine and half feminine – on one side the soft curves and draped sari of a woman, on the other the supple strength and chiseled features of a man. This is to remind us that in every man or woman who has discovered the divinity within, the best of what is feminine and the best of what is masculine come together. Great figures like Francis of Assisi, Mahatma Gandhi, and Teresa of Avila appeal deeply to men and women alike.

> *. . . never seeking itself. For in whatever*
> *instance a person seeketh himself, there he*
> *falleth from love.*

Nobody who is trying to get purely personal satisfaction out of a relationship is in love. Thomas a Kempis puts it even more strongly by saying that that person "*falleth* from love": he gets hurt, and he hurts others too. In a sense, this is the central paradox of life: the more we seek our own pleasure, our own way, the more unhappy we become. Again, Meister Eckhart said it magnificently: "Where creature stops, there God begins. All God wants of you is for you to go out of yourself in respect of your creatureliness and let God be God in you."

To borrow the language of contemporary science, the man or woman who has no self-will is a kind of superconductor. It's a powerful metaphor, because in superconductivity electricity encounters virtually no resistance. Scientists and technologists tell us that superconductivity can allow for unheard-of technological progress – for example, levitating trains – achieved with small machines, little pollution, and noninvasive technology. Similarly, when a person has no self-will, he or she is always aware of the unity of life. Whomever he meets he will meet at a deep level. No barrier can come in her way. That's why such a person is able to console others – comfort them, nourish them, and strengthen their relationships.

Love is circumspect, humble . . .

In an interview with Mother Teresa of Calcutta a reporter said to her, "Humble as you are, it must still be an extraordinary thing to be a vehicle of God's grace in the world." She answered, "But it is *his* work. I think God wants to show his greatness by using our nothingness. I am like a little pencil in his hand. That is all." Mahatma Gandhi always claimed to be no more than an ordinary man – and he *was* ordinary, until he followed the call coming from within. Then he became, after many years of transformation, a powerful force for good in the world.

In my own life, grace came through both my mother and my grandmother. My grandmother was like a tree of which my mother was the flower, and to the extent my own life has borne fruit, all the credit goes to them. In a sense, I have done nothing but live out what began with them.

As your meditation deepens, you will come to see in how many beautiful ways others have shaped your life and set your feet on the path. It's the mark of the self-realized man or woman that like Mother Teresa, they will refuse to be congratulated on anything they have accomplished.

. . . and upright, not yielding to softness . . .

Saint Francis was described as almost fragile in appearance, delicate as a reed. Gandhi weighed only a hundred pounds at the time of his death. And my grandmother was probably smaller than either of them. Yet when they took a stand, no one on earth could move them. The combination of tenderness and toughness made them irresistible. To be tender without toughness is sentimentality. To be tough but not tender is cruelty. But in a great spiritual figure, the two qualities are perfectly balanced. To be gentle you first have to be secure.

. . . or to levity, nor attending to vain things.

It's always remarkable to me to observe in restaurants the gravity with which people study the menu: the thoughtful frown on the forehead as the choices are made, the close consultation with a friend who has eaten there before. And often, if there is a slight discrepancy between the dream as it is offered and the reality on the plate, the waiter is told to go back and restore our faith.

It is the same in the department store: the utter absorption with which people exercise their sacred right to choose . . . between stripes and plaids, synthetic fibers and natural ones, double-breasted and classic . . .

These are all "vain things," in the vocabulary of Thomas a Kempis, not worthy of our serious attention; and in giving ourselves over to them, we weaken our capacity to love. That is why Jesus says, "Lay not up for yourselves treasures upon earth, where moth and rust doth corrupt and where thieves break through and steal." Don't chase after things that come and go; settle only for what abides. Why store things that get rusty almost overnight? Why try to possess things which might be stolen tomorrow? Instead, why not have things that increase with the passage of time? "Lay up for yourselves treasures in heaven."

We're all susceptible to those advertisements that enjoin, "Watch your money grow." But the mystics remind us that while money may grow, the satisfaction we get from it shrinks. Mother Teresa of Calcutta said in an interview that from her observations of life, the more money people have, the poorer and more insecure they become. That is because our real wealth is not money but desire. Once we come to realize this, we understand the importance of investing our desire-capital well. One of my responsibilities as a spiritual teacher is to play the part of a wise stockbroker. When I see someone investing heavily in short-term pleasures, I say, "Sell out now!" Don't hold on to worthless certificates in the hope that they'll go up in value. Build yourself a solid portfolio, full of high-yielding investments. Buy all the shares you can in selfless living.

It is sober, chaste, steady, quiet . . .

So much of what passes for joy in today's world is really only excitement – and once you have begun to experience even for a moment what it is to have a still mind, you will understand that excitement is a form of pain. That is why the exultant grin of the lottery winner can so easily be taken for a grimace.

The wellsprings of joy and fulfillment are within, and they can only be discovered by the man or woman who has gone beyond pleasure as well as pain. It takes many years to achieve this, because the entire nervous system must be reconditioned. It has to be strengthened to withstand the tremendous impact of the flood of love and joy that will one day surge up from within.

There is no contradiction between a sober, quiet exterior and an interior that is full of light and love. It is a terrible misunderstanding to think mystics are killjoys or wet blankets. Mystics are *give*joys – they are *warm* blankets. When life is cold, they will wrap you in warmth. When you feel desolate or abandoned, they will remind you that you are the beloved child of God.

. . . and guarded in all the senses.

You can train your senses through meditation so effectively that when the tavern or the casino is pulling them in, you can just say "Withdraw!" and they will obey you.

Analogies from the automotive world come so naturally in modern life that I have hit upon one to explain the value of this precious skill. When you leave your car somewhere, you turn off the engine, lock it, and take the key with you. Otherwise, anybody can climb in and drive your new Volvo away. Similarly, when the desire for a double martini comes and tries to get in the driver's seat, you say, "The key is in my pocket. And that's where it's going to stay!" It's absurd to think that by acquiring this control over our senses, we are losing the joy of life. Rather, we are gaining security *and* joy.

Love is subject . . .

None of us is unemployed. All of us are born to be servants of God. We are all born on earth to make life a little better than we found it. And until we understand this and begin to carry out our job, a feeling of frustration will always haunt us. In whatever capacity – teacher, carpenter, doctor, engineer, gardener, computer programmer – we become fulfilled when we use our talent, our training, our time and energy, for the benefit of all, without questioning what we'll get in return.

. . . and obedient to its superiors . . .

Thomas a Kempis was writing in a monastic context to people who had taken the threefold vow of poverty, chastity, and obedience. Most of us are not members of monastic communities, but we are engaged in essentially the same effort to eradicate self-will as Thomas's fellow monks. For this reason I would like to offer a set not of vows but of watchwords for twentieth-century aspirants.

First, where poverty is concerned, I like to recall a verse in Sanskrit composed by Bhartrihari, a poet who, according to tradition, was a king who renounced his kingdom to take up the spiritual life. He said, "You are rich, and your clothes are of silk; I live in a cottage and wear simple clothes. Yet I am content with what I have; these disparities are deceiving. Poverty is when one's desire for things is never satisfied. When the mind is at peace, who is the poor man and who the rich?"

Spiritual poverty, in other words, is a state of mind rather than the state of your bank balance. That is why instead of telling my friends to embrace lives of poverty, I suggest *simplicity.* There is a beautiful art to consciously reducing your needs in accordance with the limitations of our small planet. "Live simply," says the trenchant slogan I see on some bumpers now, "so that others may simply live."

Second, chastity. In all the monastic traditions of the world, the vow of chastity is a time-honored approach to mastering sexual drives. For those who choose to live in a lasting, loving relationship, I suggest an alternative that can be much more challenging and much more fulfilling: to live in unswerving loyalty to your partner. The conditioning of life today makes this exceedingly difficult, but the rewards are enormous.

The third traditional monastic vow, which Thomas a Kempis refers to here, is obedience – and here I like to set forth the ideal of *unity,* putting the needs of the whole before our own personal satisfaction. When it comes to our own needs we must always be ready to bend: to compromise at the periphery while standing firm at the center.

The self-willed person is rigid, like someone with only one bone. Give him a push and he falls and breaks into a dozen pieces. The Lord has given us all these bones for a reason: we can bend in every direction, and that is our glory. It is our capacity to bend when necessary to accommodate others, knowing we will not break, that gives us security.

During the rainy season in northern India, the Ganges River rises from the Himalayas and pours down the mountains in torrents, uprooting huge trees as if they were matchsticks. Our scriptures say that one day a sage saw this terrific sight and asked, "Mother Ganga, how is it that you uproot these mighty trees but leave the rushes and grasses to flourish?" She replied, "Big trees cannot bend, so I have to uproot them. The rushes and grasses bend and let me pass."

Those who are strong enough to bend their will gracefully to benefit others, to lower themselves effortlessly to serve others, have little to fear from the fierce currents and turmoil of life. They will be tested, true, but they will survive and flourish.

. . . to itself mean and despised . . .

We needn't let Thomas's medieval language alarm us here. He is saying only what Gandhi said: "I am the most ambitious man in the world: I want to make myself zero."

. . . unto God devout and thankful:
trusting and hoping always in him, even
then when God imparteth no relish of
sweetness unto it.

Every one of us at times cries out, "Oh, the Lord hasn't come! I've been at this five months, ten months, three years, and he still isn't here! What's the matter?"

At times like this every great mystic will counsel patience. And if we are sincere, we do try to be patient – at least with a kind of impatient patience.

I think it is for our safety that the Lord doesn't come in a helicopter. He comes in a bullock cart, trundling along the back roads, because he knows that to a certain extent we have to suffer and reflect and learn.

Once you've learned to take a long view of spiritual development, you begin to see certain patterns and trust them. Progress in meditation doesn't follow a straight line. It comes in fits and starts, and typically a leap forward is preceded by a period of doubt – not so much of the path itself as of your own capacity to stick it out.

This kind of uncertainty can bring enormous suffering, because you know now that nothing else on earth can satisfy you.

For without sorrow none liveth
in love.

God is love, but God can also be a tyrant – for our good. When we go after things that can only bring insecurity and ugliness, it is out of his great love that the Lord may hit us hard. On occasion he is forced to take up what G. K. Chesterton called the "holy hammer." It goes against his nature for the Lord to hurt us, but often there is no other way he can draw our attention. If he tries to tap us on the shoulder, we pay no heed. If he says from within, "Hey, you!" we plug our ears in a frenzy of activity. But one good, hard blow – and we listen!

For the good student, a gentle rap on the knuckles can be enough. But most of us just go on taking the blows until someone close to us has to whisper, "I say, you aren't doing so well. You're always hostile and agitated, and your knuckles are all scraped and swollen!" We might try to say, "Oh, I was born like this. I can take it." But inside, we know the pain is mounting. In traditional language, the Lord within is trying to tell us that we've been making wrong choices. But it is just as accurate to use more modern language: wrong choices bring painful consequences. "If you think or act with a selfish thought," the Buddha says, "suffering will follow you, as the wheel of a bullock cart follows the foot of the bullock."

Training the mind to avoid repeating wrong choices is rather like giving the body a vaccine. The reason you don't get chicken pox more than once, scientists tell us, is that the body has a kind of biochemical memory. After one attack of a virus, the immune system becomes educated: the next time it sees that enemy cell, it releases its own killer cells to swallow it up. It is because of this precious capacity of the body that vaccines are effective. One small lesson – a very light case of the disease – and no second lesson is needed; the immune system is ready. In the same way, we should be able to learn from a light run-in with jealousy or resentment not to contract the disease again.

Viruses, of course, are particularly cunning creatures. They can put on all kinds of fancy clothes. We get flu over and over because the immune system doesn't recognize the many viruses to be the same old flu: a false nose, a wig, a changed walk, and the immune system is deceived. Similarly, many of the mistakes we make are subtle; they overtake us before we see them coming, and every time they come they look a little different. But here, too, we are given some margin for learning. In time we should be able to see through all the disguises and recognize self-will and selfishness for what they really are. Then we remember the harm they do us. In this sense, meditation is like a long process of immunization. You close your eyes, make a fist, find the vein in your mind, and in goes the vaccine: "Where there is hatred, let me sow love; where there is injury, pardon . . ."

To put it very simply, the purpose of the pain we undergo in life is to help us go beyond pain.

He that is not prepared to suffer all things, and to stand to the will of his Beloved, is not worthy to be called a lover of God.

More than twenty-five years ago I was invited to the Spiritual Life Institute in Sedona, Arizona, to give a series of talks, and while Christine and I were there we were taken to a beautiful chapel on a hillside. Cactus flowers were in bloom all around, and the deep red of the rocks and sand stood out magnificently against the strong blue of the desert sky. We walked in the front door and found ourselves standing before a life-sized crucifix carved by a sculptor who had wanted us to receive the agony of the Passion in full measure. I wasn't prepared for it, so the suffering went straight in. When I saw the elongated body with outstretched arms, the hollow eyes and the lips parted in pain, it was as if Christ himself were pleading to us, "Why don't you take me off the cross?"

Wherever we see anyone suffering, Christ is telling us, "That is me you see – your Beloved." Jesus on the cross says, "Help me!" when he sees how much suffering we have caused all over the world, by striking out against one another and conniving at exploitation.

Many of the great Christian mystics heard this cry from their Lord and found themselves rushing to his aid. Catherine of Genoa felt herself almost thrown headlong out of her privileged existence as a Genoese aristocrat into the slums of the city, where she nursed the victims of plague, syphilis, and poverty for nearly thirty years. Catherine of Siena spent most of her much shorter life struggling to heal the wounds of an entire country that was torn by war, corruption, and schism. And today, Mother Teresa of Calcutta lives out her love for Christ in tender service to suffering humanity all over the world. The same interview I mentioned earlier included this exchange:

"What did you do this morning?"

"We prayed."

"When?"

"At half past four."

"And after prayer?"

"We continue to pray through our work by doing it with Jesus, for Jesus, and to Jesus. That helps us put our whole heart and soul into doing it. Serving Jesus in the dying, the crippled, the mentally ill, the unwanted, the unloved – they are Jesus in disguise."

When love reaches its highest pitch, it is eager to embrace any amount of suffering for the sake of the beloved, and it feels that suffering as joy. In the furthest reaches of prayer, the human being enters a mysterious world where by a strange kind of alchemy, two distinctions are dissolved. One is the distinction between joy and sorrow; the other is the distinction between oneself and the rest of life. This is the supreme mystery enshrined by all the world's religions. It is the mystery Saint John of the Cross was trying to convey when he spoke of "the wound that burns to heal." Meister

Eckhart says it most plainly: "He who suffers for love does not suffer, for all suffering is forgot."

A lover ought to embrace willingly all that is hard and distasteful for the sake of his Beloved, and not to turn away from him for any contrary accidents.

No one has etched this great truth into human consciousness more indelibly than Francis of Assisi. The chroniclers describe how one day, late in his life, Francis went to visit a mountain – *his* mountain, in fact, because a devoted follower had actually deeded it to Francis for his Order to use. The mountain was called La Verna, and legend claimed that the deep crevasses running down its sides had opened up in a great earthquake on the day Christ was crucified. Francis knew he was near his death and wanted to draw as close as he could to the Master he had served so passionately. So that he could be completely alone, he established himself on a rocky ledge of the mountain which could be reached only by crossing a single log. He gave his companion, Brother Leo, permission to bring him water and recite matins once a day, but otherwise he remained alone. More than a month passed while he prayed and waited. At last he entered a state of deep contemplation and asked the Lord for two graces before he should die. The first was that he feel in his body and soul the suffering Christ had undergone at Golgotha. The second was that he feel in his heart the exceeding love for all that had brought Christ there to be crucified.

Francis remained a long time in prayer. Then, the chroniclers say, "Through love and through compassion he was wholly changed into Jesus." At one and the same instant, he felt exceeding great joy and unspeakable grief. The suffering he felt was so great that it invaded his body, and blood began to flow out of his palms and feet and side as it had from the wounds of Jesus in the Passion. Francis concealed these wounds as best he could, but his followers observed them – saw that he could no longer place the soles of his feet on the ground, and that his garments were perpetually blood-stained. He carried with him, too, the marks of Jesus in his heart: "a burning flame of divine love."

To love, Saint Francis teaches, *is* to feel pain. When you have attained full awareness of God, you have the joy of being able to relieve pain, but the pain itself you cannot escape. That is why Jesus is called the Man of Sorrows. Gandhi, too, was a man of sorrow, and that is why he was a man of joy. He was a man in pain; that is why he was a man in love. To be a lover is to be a martyr. If you are a lover of all life, you feel a dagger in your heart wherever people are treated cruelly, wherever any living creature is in pain. You suffer the pain, but your suffering releases endless energy that flows forth in creative action. Saint Francis's love still floods the world, and Gandhi's love still pours into it like the Ganges itself.

Martin Luther King, Jr., said, "If you have not found the cause for which you are willing to lay down your life, you have not yet begun to live." Words like these strike us with terror, because we believe if we do find such a cause, then the Lord could well say tomorrow morning, "Okay, put your head on the block." But in fact, it is often when we are prepared to give up our life for the sake of the Lord that he wants us to live long, because then we are able to serve him.

When spiritual teachers talk about meditation, they often speak of putting an end to sorrow. It is easy to misunderstand this. "Don't you feel any grief, then?" I am sometimes asked. And of course I do. It is not that I do not feel pain; but the pain that is in my heart today comes of seeing the pain of others. All my capacity for sorrow, which I used to waste on myself, has been turned into compassion. And the joy that comes of being able to relieve pain never goes away. In the deepest stages of meditation, when I became aware that everybody's suffering is mine and that I had developed a capacity to help, I began to find an unlimited joy.

As a child I had always been sensitive to suffering, but whenever I asked myself what I could do to relieve suffering around me, the answer had always been, "Nothing. You're too small." But my capacity to feel suffering grew with deepening meditation, little by little. And my desire to relieve suffering kept deepening with my capacity to feel it. Today I know that once a person becomes one with the Lord, he or she feels the suffering of all. Yet there is a simultaneity of suffering and joy, far beyond the duality of pleasure and pain. Now I am prepared to face any amount of pain, because the Lord has granted me the immense desire to relieve the suffering of others.

When we change our way of seeing – when, after

years of spiritual striving, we begin to see with the eyes of love – we will live in a different world. If we give others deep respect and trust, and bear all suffering with patience and internal toughness, we will find ourselves in a compassionate universe. The eyes of love see the core of goodness in the hearts of others, and that is how I see the world today. It is not that I fail to see suffering and sorrow. But I understand the laws of life and see its unity everywhere. All I ask is that I may ever see this vision, and ever serve the Lord of Love in every living creature.

Thomas a Kempis

The Wonderful Effects
of Divine Love

1

*Ah, Lord God, thou holy lover of my soul, when
thou comest into my heart, all that is within me
shall rejoice.*

*Thou art my glory and the exultation of my
heart: thou art my hope and refuge in the day
of my trouble.*

2

*But because I am as yet weak in love,
and imperfect in virtue, I have need to be
strengthened and comforted by thee; visit me
therefore often, and instruct me with all holy
discipline.*

*Set me free from evil passions, and heal my heart
of all inordinate affections; that being inwardly
cured and thoroughly cleansed, I may be made*

fit to love, courageous to suffer, steady to persevere.

3

Love is a great thing, yea, a great and thorough good; by itself it makes every thing that is heavy, light; and it bears evenly all that is uneven.

For it carries a burden which is no burden, and makes every thing that is bitter, sweet and tasteful.

The noble love of Jesus impels a man to do great things, and stirs him up to be always longing for what is more perfect.

Love desires to be aloft, and will not be kept back by any thing low and mean.

Love desires to be free, and estranged from all worldly affections, that so its inward sight may not be hindered; that it may not be entangled by any temporal prosperity, or by any adversity subdued.

Nothing is sweeter than love, nothing more courageous, nothing higher, nothing wider, nothing more pleasant, nothing fuller nor better in heaven and earth; because love is born of God, and cannot rest but in God, above all created things.

4

He that loveth, flyeth, runneth, and rejoiceth; he is free, and cannot be held in.

He giveth all for all, and hath all in all; because he resteth in One highest above all things, from whom all that is good flows and proceeds.

He respecteth not the gifts, but turneth himself above all goods unto the Giver.

Love oftentimes knoweth no measure, but is fervent beyond all measure.

Love feels no burden, thinks nothing of trouble, attempts what is above its strength, pleads no excuse of impossibility; for it thinks all things lawful for itself and all things possible.

It is therefore able to undertake all things, and it completes many things, and warrants them to take effect, where he who does not love, would faint and lie down.

5

Love is watchful, and sleeping slumbereth not.

Though weary, it is not tired; though pressed, it is not straitened; though alarmed, it is not confounded; but as a lively flame and burning torch, it forces its way upwards, and securely passes through all.

If any man love, he knoweth what is the cry of this voice.

For it is a loud cry in the ears of God, the mere ardent affection of the soul, when it saith, 'My God, my love, thou art all mine, and I am all thine.'

6

Enlarge thou me in love, that with the inward palate of my heart I may taste how sweet it is to love, and to be dissolved, and as it were to bathe myself in thy love.

Let me be possessed by love, mounting above myself, through excessive fervor and admiration.

Let me sing the song of love, let me follow thee,

my Beloved, on high; let my soul spend itself in thy praise, rejoicing through love.

Let me love thee more than myself, nor love myself but for thee: and in thee all that truly love thee, as the law of love commandeth, shining out from thyself.

7

Love is active, sincere, affectionate, pleasant and amiable; courageous, patient, faithful, prudent, long-suffering, manly, and never seeking itself.

For in whatever instance a person seeketh himself, there he falleth from love.

Love is circumspect, humble, and upright; not yielding to softness, or to levity, nor attending to vain things; it is sober, chaste, steady, quiet, and guarded in all the senses.

Love is subject, and obedient to its superiors, to itself mean and despised, unto God devout and thankful, trusting and hoping always in him, even then when God imparteth no relish of sweetness unto it: for without sorrow, none liveth in love.

8

He that is not prepared to suffer all things, and to stand to the will of his Beloved, is not worthy to be called a lover of God.

A lover ought to embrace willingly all that is hard and distasteful, for the sake of his Beloved; and not to turn away from him for any contrary accidents.

Afterword

by Carol Flinders

Like a vast river with a wide and fertile flood plain, *The Imitation of Christ* has touched and nourished more lives, but for the Bible itself, than any other book in the Western world. Written in the context of Catholic monasticism, its depth and power are nonetheless felt universally. Saint Therese of Lisieux memorized it in its entirety, and Saint Ignatius of Loyola commended it for daily study. The New England Quaker and reformer John Woolman seems to have read it with deep appreciation. "In reading his writings I have believed him to be a man of true Christian spirit." (That may sound like faint praise, but for a Quaker of Woolman's time to praise a Roman Catholic in *any* fashion took some doing!) *The Imitation of Christ* was the book that Dag Hammarskjöld carried with him on the flight that ended in his death. Dame Edith Cavell read it nightly, and it was cherished by the martyred Protestant minister Dietrich Bonhoeffer. In the Coptic monasteries of Egypt today, it is a treasured spiritual manual. The book has found its way into fiction, too: Dame Agatha Christie's Miss Marple reads a chapter each night, and at the critical moment when George Eliot's heroine Maggie Tulliver has nowhere left to turn, it is *The Imitation of Christ* that bears her up.

So beguiling are the bends and twists of this great river,

and the charm of the towns it passes through, that we forget to look for the tiny wellspring in the high country where it starts. Indeed, the location of that wellspring is a vexed issue. Some remarkably vitriolic essays have been written on the probable authorship of this spiritual classic! Part of the difficulty is that the book is more a distillation than an original production. On every page one finds quotations or paraphrases from Scripture, from the church fathers, and from writings of the first members of the Brothers of the Common Life. We have no manuscript copy, moreover, on which anybody has actually *claimed* authorship.

There is little to go on, and as Easwaran reminds us in his introduction, Thomas himself asked that we "search not who spoke this or that, but mark what is spoken." Still, for many of us authorship is a compelling matter. When we love a book, we want to know about the life behind it. Is it of a piece with the book? Besides, it isn't just the cumulative wisdom of all those citations that makes the *Imitation* a perennial favorite; it is that *voice* – so warm and compassionate, despite the gravity of the teachings; so tender and yet, here and there, just a little wry.

Fortunately for those of us who care, the scholarly world has reached accord on the question of authorship. Names like Jean Gerson and Saint Bernard of Clairvaux are no longer proposed with any seriousness. Thomas a Kempis is the recognized author, so long as we understand that the whole notion of authorship didn't mean in his time what it does today – particularly where spiritual writings were concerned. When a man or woman was able to inspire others, by spoken as well as by written word, it wasn't thought to be through any special gift of their own.

The Holy Spirit was working through them. The interesting question is, then, what is it about such a human being that *allows* the Holy Spirit to work through him or her?

Typically, to find the answer to this question, we do best to stay clear of the more tumultuous population centers of times past, looking instead to quieter places: backwater towns, lively with the warmth of long-standing relationships, slow-paced and simple: places like Ruysbroeck, the village where Jan of Ruysbroeck was born; Norwich, the English cathedral town where Julian lived and wrote; and Deventer, another cathedral town, this one set in the Yssel Valley of what is now the Netherlands . . .

Thomas Hamerken was thirteen, maybe only twelve years old – for the chronicles don't jibe – when he traveled a hundred miles or so from a tiny village outside Cologne to the prosperous, busy town of Deventer. The year was 1392. His father's name meant "he with a little hammer"; he was probably a carpenter. Kempen was the name of the village from which he came, and it was the village, not the father, which would be remembered for having given Thomas to the world.

Handsome brick buildings lined the busy streets of Deventer, streets that were laid out around the stone cathedral of Saint Lebwen, built six hundred years before to honor the Anglo-Saxon missionary who had first brought the word of Christ to this part of Europe. Deventer was considerably quieter than nearby Rotterdam, but culturally it was much more active: the recorded demand for books during the fifteenth century is astonishing. Everything Thomas saw when he arrived there was new to him, but not unknown, because his older brother John had told him all about it – had told him, too, about the cathedral school he would be attending, and, most glowingly of all, about the Brothers of the Common Life, who were doing so much to smooth the way for young scholars. John had been through the Deventer schools himself, drawn like other boys from throughout the Rhineland by the schools' excellent reputation. In time he had been drawn still more irresistibly by the sanctity and fellowship of the Brotherhood itself. From the dormitories maintained by the Brothers for boys like himself, it had been an easy step into the Augustinian monastery at nearby Windesheim, established just eight years before by the founder of the Brothers of the Common Life, Geert Groote.

Both the Hamerken sons had taken their earliest lessons from their mother, who ran a small school in her home. But village schools equipped a child only to read and write. The "chapter schools," also called "Latin schools," were located in larger towns. There boys between nine and fifteen would learn Latin and dialectics in preparation for the "trivium" and the "quadrivium" of one of the great universities. Even if he were only twelve, then, Thomas was far from being the youngest scholar to be making his own way in the world.

The schools were generally run by the town governments, but there was no general system for boarding the students. A popular sentiment did prevail – "A bed, a beer, and a stew for the love of God" – and most of the pious people of Deventer complied; but boys need more than one meal a day, so many ended up begging. Their scholarly performance under those circumstances could not have been first-rate.

All this has to be put in perspective, of course. Historian Barbara Tuchman points out that *most* little boys of the period were packed off in one direction or another by their seventh year: the nobleman's son to a friend's castle, to learn the fine arts of thrashing and bashing; the peasant's son to someone else's shop or farm to be apprenticed. "If children survived till age seven," she explains, "their recognized life began, more or less as miniature adults."

Still, no matter how impassively the world may have regarded all those children, children they still were. "When I was a child," Saint Paul reminds us, "I spake as a child, I understood as a child," and it seems fair to impute to that young boy in a strange town feelings of confusion and apprehension – particularly when we find out he hadn't a penny to his name.

Thomas a Kempis was one of life's lucky ones, though, and he never stopped being grateful for it. For on his way into Deventer, he had dropped in at the monastery at Windesheim to see his older brother, and John had told him to go see the vicar, Florent Radewijns, as soon as he got into town.

Foremost among the Brothers now that Groote himself was gone – in fact, Groote's chosen successor and the only one of his associates whom he had asked to take holy orders – Radewijns was a man of great spiritual stature. Unhesitatingly, he took the boy into his vicarage and lodged him there until he found suitable quarters with "a devout matron." Seeing that the boy had no money, he provided books and paid his tuition.

Increasingly, the Brothers had made the protection and nurturing of these young boys their special apostolate: finding homes with good families, making sure they could afford books, and finally even setting up well-supervised dormitories where the boys got not just a beer, a bed, and a stew, but help with their homework and spiritual guidance as well. Did they need income? The Brothers instructed them in the valued art of manuscript copying, and found them work, too. Florent Radewijns appears to have been the moving force behind this concern and the work it fueled.

Years later, Thomas a Kempis would write a biography of Radewijns to inspire his own novices to greater spiritual efforts, and his deeply felt gratitude infuses the work. "Master John Boheme," he tells us,

> who was Rhetor of the scholars, was a friend to Florentius [Radewijns]. And when the time to pay the fees was come, each scholar brought what was justly due, and I also put my fee into his hand. . . . He, having some knowledge of me and aware that I was under the care of Florentius, said, "Who gave thee this money?" And I answered, "My lord Florentius." "Then go," said he, "take back his money, since for love of him I will take nothing from thee." So I took back the money again . . . and said, "The Master hath given back my fee for love of thee." And Florentius said, "I thank him and will repay him, after another fashion with gifts more excellent than money."

In the years to come, Thomas would have considerable contact with Radewijns. He carried messages for the revered man and often attended to his simple needs at mealtimes. He describes his mentor in choir:

> He did not gaze about with wandering eyes, but stood very quietly turning towards the altar with all restraint and reverence. . . . And as often as I saw my Master Florentius standing there, I was careful not to chatter.

. . . Once on a time it happened when I was standing
near him in the choir that he turned to share our book for
the chanting, and he, standing behind me, put his hands
upon my shoulder – but I stood still, hardly daring to
move, bewildered with gratification at so great an
honor."

What a sweet-natured, entirely devout soul Thomas a
Kempis appears to have been: "simple" in the most exalted
sense of the word; seamless, absolutely undivided. His life
is virtually without event. From the dormitories of the
Brothers, just like his brother John, he would move into
the monastery at Mount Saint Agnes, and there live for virtually all his ninety-one years (ninety-one in those days!).
He was an exceptional copyist and the composer of a great
many spiritual works besides *The Imitation of Christ.* He
held the office of subprior, which made him master of the
novices, for years on end. A brief stint as provisioner
proved, apparently, calamitous, and it's amusing how
much satisfaction his biographers have taken from that. A
fellow monastic leaves us this description: "As he meditated, the tips of his toes alone touched the floor, the rest
of his body . . . lifted heavenwards, whither his soul
tended with all its desires."

One yearns for a more telling, more *personal* glimpse of
Thomas a Kempis, but his official biography is disap-
pointingly vague. The only real insights we have into his
personality emerge out of reading the biographies *he*
wrote of other members of his spiritual circle. These por-
traits were gathered into a volume called *The Founders of
the New Devotion.* Insofar as he'll ever be, the "real"
Thomas is here. Not that you get any direct information
about his own life – he was a monk, after all, and in a sense

monks *have* no personal life. Still, he is a writer, and it's often the small things a writer or a photographer or painter focuses upon that tell you who he or she really is. So beautifully do these other lives shine through that you come away feeling that Thomas's greatest gift is to be a perfect medium, clear and pure.

Thomas offers many proofs, for instance, of Florent Radewijns' sanctity. None, though, is sweeter than this:

> So too, in the month of May, the season when the wild herbs that are used as medicaments have their highest virtue, the good Father did not forget his poor; knowing that many were weak, ulcerous, and full of sores, he made them to come to his house upon an appointed day and hour to receive certain medicines, and to have their bodies bathed in warm water infused with aromatic herbs. And when they had been thoroughly bathed and washed he made ready for each a most cleanly bed for sudorific treatment. And after receiving a cup of wine, and some words of comfort, they went away with great joy to their own homes. . . .

A delight in the natural world that is almost Franciscan pervades his accounts. He plays with etymologies for Radewijns' name. *Florentius*, he speculates, could mean *flores colligens*, "the gatherer of flowers," for he had gathered so many clerks and Brothers "in the flower of their age" to serve and love the Lord. He takes an episode from Radewijns' youth, so very slight that you wonder how he even chanced to hear it:

> It happened upon a time that he was invited with many others to a marriage, and when they were upon the way together, being most eager to pleasure his friends and to make merry with them, he did as follows for their gratification: cutting down green branches from the

trees, he took them and embowered those who sat in the carriage in such wise as greatly to win their favor.

Thomas goes on to allegorize – this was the high Middle Ages, after all – but what we retain is the image itself, of the young man so eager to please his friends, slashing away at the hedgerows, clambering over the carriage to pile up the greenery, teasing the laughing couple as they disappear inside a leafy canopy . . . doing exactly what the moment called for, for such is always the genius of deeply spiritual individuals.

Of the author of *The Imitation of Christ,* then, we still have only the faintest sketch. But as I've suggested, the *Imitation* is not so much the work of a single man as it is of an entire spiritual movement, and of that movement we can pull together quite a clear picture.

As you turn the pages of *Founders,* you get a feeling not only for the individuals themselves but also for the extraordinary atmosphere Thomas Hamerken had walked into there in Deventer. "Pear seeds grow into pear trees," said Meister Eckhart, "and God-seeds into God-trees." Thomas a Kempis was a God-seed, without question. But for his life to have unfolded as perfectly and fragrantly as it did, the soil had to be perfectly prepared, too.

Historian Barbara Tuchman has asked us to see in the Europe of the fourteenth century a mirror of our own times. Her best-selling book *A Distant Mirror* is subtitled "The Calamitous Fourteenth Century." The catalog of woes is stunning: war, plague, schism, oppressive taxation, bad government, insurrection, brigandage. Even the weather seemed to be pitted against humankind, for climatic shifts that began in the early part of the century made for lower temperatures, heavy rains, and a shortened growing season. In the wake of all this, famine spread, weakening the population so that it would be all the more susceptible to the plague.

One can set forth the essentials of Thomas a Kempis's life with almost no reference to any of these events. As a cloistered monk, his daily life was spent entirely with individuals who, like himself, had turned away from the world and put all their attention to their own reconstruction. By temperament he was reclusive, never so happy as when, in his own words, he had "a little book in a little nook." What he wrote and did could have been written and done in almost any century.

But just one generation earlier, the founder of Thomas's spiritual community was living a radically different kind of life, one much more in the roiling, passionate, and anguished tradition of Saint Augustine. Geert Groote, founder of the Brothers and Sisters of the Common Life, was an enormously appealing, highly idiosyncratic figure of tremendous energy and talent – a man who did nothing, ever, by half measures. Geert Groote was a man absolutely of his own times. In contrast to Thomas's life, Groote's was shaped by events and forces that were quite without precedent.

First, and most spectacular, was the Black Death, which swept through Europe in wave after terrible wave throughout the second half of the fourteenth century, reducing the population by a third within the first three years, and ultimately by half. Groote's own parents died in the first assault, and he himself would succumb to one of the later epidemics. The terrible swiftness of the disease (typically one died within three to five days of contracting it), its ugliness, and the inconceivable suffering it brought – the horror of lifeless bodies that amassed too rapidly to be buried, the decimation of entire towns and the emptying of whole monasteries – seems to have benumbed the minds of those who witnessed it. Barbara Tuchman points out that chroniclers say astonishingly little about the plague, and speculates that it simply overwhelmed them. Some things, perhaps, just cannot *be* assimilated.

Second, the church itself was in a state of profound disarray. The Great Schism did not officially begin until 1378 (ending in 1417), but it had been a long time developing. The years of the dual papacy, and the preceding period as well, were profoundly demoralizing to the entire Christian world. The division cut across countries and cities, then villages, and ultimately families.

Overlaid across all of this, and continuing through five generations, there was the Hundred Years' War, begun in 1339. Fought, technically, between France and Britain, it drained and savaged most of northern Europe before it ended in 1453.

Geert Groote was born in the year 1340. He was just seven the year ships from the Black Sea port of Caffa docked in Messina, Sicily, carrying a deadly cargo from the East. By the next year, 1348, the bubonic plague was advancing northward across Europe, and the town of Deventer was bracing itself in the few small ways it could. The hospital was enlarged, the public cleansing department was set to work, and some simple disinfectants, like white vinegar, were stored in the city hall.

Not that anyone put much store by these measures. This was the Black Death, an implacable and terrible judgment against humanity. Better to ready your soul than the hospital. The plague struck Deventer in 1350, and by the end of summer both Geert's parents were gone. Under relatives' guardianship, Geert resumed his schooling when the town returned to relative normalcy. He studied at the same chapter school Thomas a Kempis would attend forty years later. At fifteen he went off to Paris for further studies. He would have been accompanied, one can be sure, by a trusty manservant, for Geert lived most certainly at the privileged end of the social scale. His inheritance was ample, and he spent freely – entertaining his friends and wearing the showiest, most elegant clothing to be had.

Groote was an unusually able student. Normally the Master of Arts degree would have required seven years of residence and the age of twenty. Groote took his at just eighteen, with only three years in residence. This degree equipped him to teach everywhere, and allowed him to continue his own formal education in medicine, law, or theology. Indeed, he continued in all three! For the next ten years he was truly a professional student, not only in Paris but in Cologne and Prague as well, teaching part-time while he studied, so avid for learning that no one line of study would content him.

His degrees had endowed him with mastery in the liberal arts. Eventually he would feel most at home in the practice of law, but immediately after receiving his degree he applied himself to the natural sciences, and that entailed some travel through murky waters. The study of the natural world and the study of magic – black and white – were utterly entangled at that time. The physical world was known to be infused and animated by the spirit world: you couldn't imagine trying to manipulate the one, or even understand it, without somehow propitiating the other. Astronomy and astrology were indistinguishable, and so were chemistry and alchemy.

By 1362, Groote was back in Paris, studying law and theology. The ecclesiastical infrastructure was in those days a rough equivalent to today's corporate world: a vast and complex system having as little to do with genuinely spiritual issues as the upper managerial echelons of General Motors do with building automobiles, but offering splendidly remunerative opportunities to adroit young men. Well schooled in canon law and theology, Groote could look forward to entering the service of a cardinal or officiating at one or another great cathedral, and in any case he could and did begin to apply now for "prebends," incomes attached to several different positions.

By his own reckoning and his biographers', the young Groote could be faulted on at least two counts: an urgent desire to be great in the eyes of the world and the arrogance that is almost inevitable in young people who move as swiftly and easily across the hurdles of academia as he did. He had, on the other hand, a gift for friendship. All his biographers remark his personal attractiveness. The friends he made during his student years would stand by him later, and would go to great lengths, when the time came, to assist in his conversion – to claim, in fact, chief responsibility for it.

If Groote sounds like something of a butterfly, the impression is probably wrong. He was just twenty-five years old when his townspeople called a meeting, at his house, to discuss an exceedingly delicate, persistent dispute with the city of Utrecht – a taxation question that needed to be resolved once and for all. Would Groote represent Deventer at the Papal Court in Avignon? They offered him a large sum of money to cover the expenses, but he refused the money and went on his own hook. In two years he succeeded in winning the case. Back to Paris then, surer than ever of a brilliant future as a scholar and clergyman. Two canonries fell into his hands.

Everything was in place now, by the laws that govern a particular kind of life, for a dramatic change in direction. Groote had done what he'd set out to do, seen what he'd wanted to see; and he was increasingly unhappy. Friends issued warnings: "You're frivolous, Geert – look at your clothes!" "This dabbling in sorcery – it's playing the devil's game." Perfect strangers issued oblique warnings. Finally, as in the lives of Saint Francis and Saint Teresa of Avila, a severe illness struck him and brought him close to death.

Groote's recovery coincided with his decision to reverse the direction of his life. There was an enormous amount of undoing to do, and piece by deliberate piece he fell to undoing it. Had he indeed spent a fortune on high fashion? He adopted a simple clerical habit and later would wear only the oldest, most tattered and nondescript clothing. Had he too eagerly sought wealth and office? He would resign all his prebends and finally give away even the use of his own home. Had he drawn others into the practice of astrology? He would actively speak against the dubious arts from now on. Had he . . . well, never mind, but he would avoid the company of women altogether for the remainder of his life. It was to "unmarried women devoted to God" that he signed over his house, reserving only a few small rooms at the back for himself, sealed off from the rest of the house.

Groote needed time in seclusion to consolidate all these changes, and to think out what the remainder of his life would be. He entered a Carthusian monastery and stayed – as a guest, not a novice – for three years. While there he completed a remarkable document, his *Conclusions and Propositions*. This would be a kind of blueprint for the rest of his life. It would be cherished by the Brothers, and much of it would find its way into the *Imitation*.

From the very first resolution flows all the rest: the service of God and the salvation of his soul were his principal tasks in this world. No temporal good whatsoever would impede him. Groote was not going to live out his years in a monastery. His *Propositions* were designed to allow him to live in the world while not of it. He would attend Mass every day – attentively and reverently. His only line of study now would be spiritual books, and he lists the ones he deems suitable. In food and drink and sleep, he would be abstinent: no meat, and very little wine.

In the fine points he can seem a bit fussy: "Seventh, take but one cooked pear after thy meal, and that not of inordinate size, or three of the very smallest." But the drift is clear: he would make each moment of the day *count* as he strove to remake himself in Christ's image. The overall tenor is buoyant, large-minded, and very carefully tailored to his own failings: "Likewise after the example of Bernard, utter no word by which thou mayest seem to be very religious, or endowed with knowledge." Practicality pervades: "It is better to do one action well with great deliberation than through lack thereof to be thrown out of one's course. . . . The same habit of deliberation should prevail in writing and speaking and in action also, because it is impossible to seek therein the glory of God if a man so impetuously rush into a matter that his whole strength is occupied in it. Learn then to be slow and restrained in action."

Seeking to establish himself in continual prayer, he would utter short, ejaculatory prayers, as the desert fathers had, throughout the day. From "Geert the Great," Thomas a Kempis writes, he had become "Geert the Humble." It's worth emphasizing this, because the very hallmark of the Brothers and Sisters of the Common Life was their utter humility, warmed and balanced by a heart-felt appreciation of one another.

For Groote, the *Propositions* constituted a highly personal "statement of intent," a promise to himself. Though their end result was a life virtually indistinguishable from that of the Carthusian monastery he'd been living in, they were not formal vows, and to him the distinction was all-important. He wasn't opposed to monastic orders on principle, but he was sure that a truly God-centered life could be lived anywhere. He wanted to find and live out the essentials of such a life, quite apart from institutional settings that may or may not facilitate it.

Groote's avowed intention was to lead others to God in two ways: the example of a holy life, and the active work of preaching and writing. The former he would begin immediately, closeted in relative seclusion in the back rooms of his house at Deventer, immersed in prayer and study. Living only barely "in the world," he attended Mass daily, prayed and meditated each morning, and sang the canonical hours, hard at his books the rest of the day. He lived on pea soup most of the time – it could simmer at the back of the stove untended. If he invited friends to supper, he made up for the scanty fare by reading to them from a shelf of spiritual books kept next to the table!

To expand his library, Groote borrowed books and had them copied. He would invite young clerks to his house in the evening, instruct them in the art of copying, and pay them for their work. Soon the evenings were given over more and more to spiritual discourse; out of these meetings would evolve, in time, the Brothers of the Common Life. The basis of that life, as of Groote's own, would be abandonment of earthly goods, adoption of a "common life," chastity of thought and word as well as deed, and annihilation of their own will. "Obedience" was not construed so much as obedience to a superior as rather an openness to one another – a willingness to be corrected and chastised by one another, and inspired. Groote felt these principles should be the basis of life for any follower of Christ, monastic or otherwise. And it was on this, the content of the spiritual life, that he placed all his attention. Of himself and his followers he exacted no vows, insisting instead upon a daily, individual renewal of intention which no merely external routine would supplant.

External conditions would in time force more formal definition of the Brothers and Sisters – their legal defense even – and those same conditions would help compel the formation of monasteries and convents. But Groote moved slowly and reluctantly in that direction. Never did he reject monasticism outright, but seemed rather to be trying to open out another avenue, to bring the spiritual life into the reach of more people than those called to holy orders: it troubled him that the word "religious" generally meant monastics. He sought the irreducible core.

In many ways, one is struck by similarities between Groote and Mahatma Gandhi. Groote's patched grey outer garment, his moth-eaten cap, were as much legend as Gandhi's spotless white loincloth would be. Scolded once by a friend, he tried to explain, "I do this, not because I have nothing better, but in order to conquer myself." His wheelbarrow full of books, jostled over the rough dirt roads of the Yssel Valley, were as much a trademark as the watch that Gandhi pinned to his one garment. Like Gandhi, too, he saw in manual labor a precious aid to spiritual growth. "Labor is a wonderful necessary to mankind in restoring the mind to purity." What spinning was for Gandhi's *satyagraha* movement, book copying was for the Brothers.

In the larger sense, too, the resemblance holds. The political crisis of Groote's time and place was the Great Schism. But he refused to address it directly, for he saw the schism itself as merely a symptom of much deeper ills – just as Gandhi saw British domination of India to be symptomatic of more far-reaching problems. Both men were trained lawyers, and both had a deep interest in medicine. Medical metaphors came naturally. The disturbance in the highest office of the church, said Groote, was like a severe headache, which indicated that a disease had been going on for a long time and had finally brought the body to the verge of collapse.

"But all of us are acting like inexperienced physicians," he said, "and try to remove the symptoms without taking care of the causes of the illness." For Groote, the causes were in the moral and spiritual inadequacies of the church members and clergy, and the only cure was reform at the level of individual lives: "trickle-up," very much in the Gandhian mode. To this end he would use all his training and rhetorical skills. Nor would he stay in the cities. Like Gandhi, he traveled tirelessly into the smallest villages, and like Gandhi, he was enormously well received. Like Gandhi, too, he grasped the importance of the local and the vernacular – his village preaching was in the local dialect.

His reception was phenomenally enthusiastic, in a time and place when preaching was not generally well received. Often he would speak all morning, then send his congregation home for a meal, meditate while they were gone, and address them again in the afternoon. Central to all his sermons was the theme of the imitation of Christ: in selfless love for one another, and consequent willingness to suffer ourselves to relieve the suffering of others, we conform to our Lord and become one with him. The special target of his entire preaching effort was clerical abuse, a preoccupation which grew directly out of an enormous respect for the office itself. Stung by his criticism, certain of the clergy turned on him and had him silenced, so that after only three years of active preaching he was forbidden to continue. Initially, he was devastated; he wrote of a "schism of his heart," and feelings of terrible uncertainty and indecision. Yearning to address the spiritual needs of his people, he appealed through a friend to Pope Urban VI to be reinstated.

Waiting for his appeal to be considered, he retired to a quiet estate outside of town, where he could spend long, uninterrupted hours in prayer and meditation. Almost immediately he was able to place himself again in the hands of God. Exultant, he poured his renewed trust and faith into a letter, "On Patience": to imitate Christ means to follow him in his passion, suffering if need be all the difficulties and pains inflicted on one by worldly-minded people. Many Christians are willing, he points out, to take up a cross they've made themselves, like penitential exercises, prayers and fasting; but the cross which God has made for them, the one that is really theirs, they throw down in horror.

Serene, then, he waited and busied himself in several ways. He translated parts of the Breviary into Dutch, and devoted himself for the first time to the formation of his disciples. He heard out a request on the part of some of these who wanted a more remote setting better suited for meditation. He gave his assent and selected a site near the town of Zwolle, where in two years the monastery of Mount Saint Agnes would open. This would be the home of Thomas a Kempis. Groote's biographers agree that he had several motives for approving the foundation. One was that antagonism from several monastic and mendicant orders was very high. The fact that the Brothers took no vows and lived out in the world was taken as an unspoken rebuke. Establishing a community of a recognized order, the Augustinian canons regular, should allay hostility; but in case it did not, the Brothers would have a place where they could come and be safe.

Groote seemed now to be acting out of a long view of things to come – as though, some of his biographers think, he knew his remaining time was short. He turned over his library and house at Zwolle for the use of the Brothers. Then, in August 1384, a friend contracted the plague. Groote went to care for him without hesitation, and fell ill himself. Knowing he was near death, he appointed Florent Radewijns to lead his followers. "Behold," he said with characteristic flair, "I am being called by the Lord. Augustine and Bernard are already knocking at the door." After giving his final instructions regarding the foundation at Mount St. Agnes, he died – having fallen far short, for all he could see, of what he'd intended. Soon after his death, there came from Rome the Pope's reply to his appeal. It was favorable – had he lived, he would have been licensed to preach once again.

This one man, then, whose essential act was simply to *turn himself around,* who gave himself so unrestrainedly and unabashedly – humbly and headlong – managed, in the words of Thomas, "to undertake all things, and bring many of them to pass, and warrant them to take effect." He was not a saint, except in the local and vernacular sense – sufficient entirely to the time and place he occupied. He'd begun by grooming himself for a role in the church hierarchy, but he ended instead, like Saint Francis, seeking to rebuild the church from the ground up – each brick being men and women whose very lives were Christlike.

The stones he set in place stood firm, and great things rose upon them. Mount St. Agnes was built, and the Windesheim foundation too. Under their protection, the Brothers were able to continue their apostolate with the students of Deventer. By 1460 there were some fifty congregations of Brothers and Sisters. Convents were founded also that bore the same relationship to the Sisters of the Common Life. Within a hundred years, the Windesheim chapter numbered ninety-two houses, and from this chapter there spread a far-reaching, powerful reform of convents and monasteries all over northern Europe. And finally, from that first community, Mount St. Agnes, whose site Groote himself selected, there would issue the incalculably precious and influential book *The Imitation of Christ.*

Library of Congress Cataloging-in-Publication Data:

Easwaran, Eknath.
Seeing with the eyes of love : reflections on a classic of
Christian mysticism
by Eknath Easwaran : with an afterword by Carol Flinders
p.   cm.
Meditations on liber 3, capitulum 5 (De mirabili effectu divini
amoris) of Imitatio Christi.
ISBN 0–915132–65–6 (alk. paper) : $22.00.
ISBN 0–915132–64–8 (pbk. : alk. paper) : $12.95
1. Imitatio Christi. Liber 3. Capitulum 5 – Meditations.
2. Love – Religious aspects – Christianity – Meditations.
3. Thomas a Kempis, 1380–1471.   4. Meditation.   I. Title.
BV4829.E27 1991
242—dc20   91–27913
CIP